THE
MODERN GERMAN NOVEL
1945-1965

SECOND EDITION

H. M. WAIDSON

Published for the UNIVERSITY OF HULL *by*

OXFORD UNIVERSITY PRESS

LONDON   NEW YORK   TORONTO

1971

Oxford University Press, Ely House, London W.1

GLASGOW NEW YORK TORONTO MELBOURNE WELLINGTON
CAPE TOWN SALISBURY IBADAN NAIROBI DAR ES SALAAM LUSAKA ADDIS ABABA
BOMBAY CALCUTTA MADRAS KARACHI LAHORE DACCA
KUALA LUMPUR SINGAPORE HONG KONG TOKYO

ISBN 0 19 713414 9

© *University of Hull 1971*

First edition 1959
Reprinted (with corrections) 1960
Second edition 1971

PRINTED AND BOUND IN ENGLAND BY
HAZELL WATSON AND VINEY LTD
AYLESBURY, BUCKS

FOREWORD TO THE SECOND EDITION

GERMAN narrative prose from 1945 onwards has shown itself to be very much alive, responding to the immediate issues and atmosphere of its time. If the present is often seen in the context of the past, there is a frequent questioning of tradition. Imaginative reactions have been widely varied, and can include the serene and idyllic as well as the ironic and militant.

The present volume, in attempting to give an introduction to some German novels of the period 1945–65, is offered in a somewhat different shape from the first edition, which aimed at discussing some of the fiction of the twelve years up to about 1957. After the introductory section, comment has been limited for the most part to novels published during the period chosen. The year 1965 seemed a convenient point at which to stop, though there is no wish to suggest that this point in time is of any particular significance otherwise in this context. A chapter on novels by authors who left Germany or Austria during the 1930s is followed by one on the work of a number of writers who have been roughly their contemporaries and who likewise were often established literary figures before 1945, but who for the most part remained in Central Europe. The novelists who are mentioned in Chapter Four largely became well known after 1945, though in some cases they had published earlier. Novels by some German-Swiss writers appear in a separate section, while work by those authors who have been associated with the 'Gruppe 47' has been brought together as another unit. Some of the writing of East German novelists is discussed in a further chapter.

It should perhaps be said that it has only been possible to deal with a limited amount of material. It is realized that there might well have been discussion of quite a number of novelists who are not mentioned in these chapters, and also that those authors who are talked about here are by no means always represented by the entirety of their published work during the period in question. Similarly the range of secondary literature on twentieth-century German novelists is such that it would be vain for me to hope to do justice to it. In the select bibliography the chief emphasis has been given to items to which the English-reading student might like to turn.

Swansea   H. M. Waidson
February 1971

CONTENTS

1 Introduction   1

2 'We have been forced to look around for a new basis
of living . . .'   14

3 '. . . After all there may still be a hope.'   38

4 '. . . The basic assumption is no longer the same.'   70

5 'If our small example were to keep guard . . .'   93

6 'Reality is a task . . .'   103

7 '. . . On behalf of this living together.'   128

8 Conclusion   141

Select Bibliography   147

List of Translations   163

Index   167

1 INTRODUCTION

ONE criterion which has been applied to determine the relevance of a novelist's work is the faithfulness of its portrayal of contemporary society. Since the eighteenth century the idea has become established that imaginative prose literature is primarily concerned with 'reality', 'time', the 'problems of life', and the 'actualities of every day'.[1] The majority of the great nineteenth-century novels have been realistic; they depict people, places, and situations which the reader can readily believe to have been a plausible reconstruction of something that not only the author could see, but that any other percipient person could have witnessed if he had been in comparable circumstances. The novelist's approach to his material in these circumstances is on the whole spontaneous and unproblematic. The imaginative world of Jane Austen is immediately credible; sober, dispassionate, sharply observed, and cleanly caught, a small social group is mirrored with what convinces the reader as accuracy. The larger worlds of Dickens, Thackeray, and Henry James may be less precisely rendered, but they are pictures of existing societies; there are edges, in Dickens particularly, which blur off from the empirical, but in the main the portrayals are convincing as imitations of things and behaviour which are outside the story-teller. Parallels may be found in nineteenth-century French and Russian literature. The important mid-nineteenth and later nineteenth-century German novelists are similarly realists, by and large, though of a regional, largely non-urban setting. The individualism of the nineteenth century, the widespread acceptance of the autonomy of personality, it has been suggested,[2] allowed the novel to reach a peak of vitality and originality at that time.

1 Horst Oppel (ed.), *Der moderne englische Roman*, Berlin, 1965, p. 7.
2 cf. Arno Schirokauer, 'Bedeutungswandel des Romans', in Volker Klotz (ed.), *Zur Poetik des Romans*. Darmstadt, 1965, p. 19.

If the modern English novel offers a 'bright and confusing picture',[3] it might well be argued that twentieth-century German fiction makes a similar impression. Much that is enheartening and stimulating is evidently there. If the picture presented is bewildering, this is part of its richness. There can only be a hope of giving a partial and interim description of a limited selection of some mid-twentieth-century novels in the pages that follow. But the comments made by Horst Oppel to distinguish English novelists of the present and the last centuries may well be applicable to their German contemporaries. He notices that language may no longer be used primarily in the service of communication, but as a means to fragmentary self-knowledge; that causality may give way to contingency; that there may be open endings and abrupt beginnings; that specific episodes may be illuminated, while much else is left in obscurity; that a modern novel may express its author's resignation to the impossibility of a rounded interpretation of life. The relationship between author and reader has become more complicated, since authorial omniscience is not infrequently regarded with mistrust, especially if the intervention of an author in his narrative and his manipulation of the characters becomes over-insistent.

Thomas Mann's *Buddenbrooks* belongs to the nineteenth-century mood in various ways. As a family chronicle it combines something of the approach of a German regional realist with that of a naturalist nearer the end of the century who is advocating the relevance of current scientific method for literary writing. The delineation of artistic sensibility has elements associated with an aesthetic impressionism. In its narrative methods it introduces the reader to the thoughts of the characters at will, and interpolates authorial comments and summaries freely. Published only a short time earlier than *Buddenbrooks*, Sigmund Freud's *Traumdeutung* was to point the way to an extension of realism beyond the conscious to the unconscious; if this linked up with facets of Romanticism at the beginning of the nineteenth century where phenomena associated with the unconscious mind found expression in fantasy, it could now lead to a searching questioning of the basis of

3 Horst Oppel, op. cit., p. 7.

personality too, and to a preoccupation with phases of mental processes that had been much less stressed in earlier times. But Freud himself makes frequent reference in his *Traumdeutung* to literary tradition, not least as embodied in the work of Goethe and Shakespeare. Since the neo-Romantic phase in Austria and Germany at the turn of the century the novelist's world has been less tightly confined within the bounds of earlier assumptions of everyday, common-sense realism. Thomas Mann's early stories as well as *Buddenbrooks* illustrate the problems of intellectuals and artists who cannot find a secure relationship to society. Tonio Kröger regrets the loss of spontaneity which he associates irrevocably with the pursuit of the artistic vocation:

Feeling, warm, heart-felt feeling, is always banal and unusable, and the only artistic qualities are the tensions and cold ecstasies of our degenerate, speciously artistic nervous system. . . . The gift for style, form and expression already takes for granted this cool and fastidious relationship to what is human, yes, takes for granted a certain human impoverishment and desolation. . . . The artist is finished as soon as he becomes human and begins to have feelings.
[My translation, as are all subsequent translations.]

Tonio eventually decides tentatively and wistfully to esteem loving kindness, and thereby to attempt to overcome his aloofness from ordinary life. Other central figures of Mann's writing in the first decade of the present century illustrate this attitude equally clearly, if not more so: Detlev Spinell in *Tristan*, or Gustav Aschenbach in *Der Tod in Venedig*, for instance.

Scepticism about the necessity of presenting an ordered time-sequence and the breaking-down of the coherent purposiveness of personality into a stream of consciousness that consists of a random flux of impressions are features of the experimental novel of the 1920s. Joyce, Proust, and Kafka display an analytic quality that probes into problematic aspects of experience and reflection with a searching and often disenchanted quality that is expressed in a radical manner that was less familiar to earlier generations. In 'Modern Fiction,' 1919, Virginia Woolf pleaded eloquently for an intensification of the novelist's imaginative insight:

Examine for a moment an ordinary mind on an ordinary day. The mind receives a myriad impressions—trivial, fantastic, evanescent, or ingraved with the sharpness of steel. From all sides they come, an incessant shower of innumerable atoms, and as they fall, as they shape themselves into the life of Monday or Tuesday, the accent falls differently from of old; the moment of importance came not here but there; so that, if the writer were a free man and not a slave, if he could write what he chose, not what he must, if he could base his work upon his own feeling and not upon convention, there would be no plot, no comedy, no tragedy, and no love-interest or catastrophe in the accepted style. . . . Life is not a series of gig-lamps symmetrically arranged; life is a luminous halo, a semi-transparent envelope surrounding us from the beginning of consciousness to the end. Is it not the task of the novelist to convey this varying, this unknown and uncircumscribed spirit, whatever aberration or complexity it may display?

It could be contended that this method was an extension and a heightening of the concept of realism in the novel. A causally and temporally straightforward narrative confining itself to events and people that would be generally accepted as plausible in life as a whole, and presented by an omniscient narrator, as often in the nineteenth-century novel, has been for many later authors no longer an adequate vehicle for expressing their vision. The world presented in the work of fiction should be self-contained in the manner in which it is laid before us. Franz K. Stanzel has said: 'Expressed in the most general terms, the aim of that tendency of the modern novel which has been constantly more strongly emphasized since James, Proust and Joyce is the striving towards an illusion of a comprehensive autonomy of the depicted world, towards the fiction of its independence of the author or of the narrator whom the author has pushed forward.'[4] With Joyce there is concentrated exposition of a limited facet of experience but at the same time a movement away from the individual to the typical and mythical, a return to the primitive epic but in a self-conscious form. This tendency can also be seen in the later work of Thomas Mann.[5]

4 Horst Oppel, op. cit., p. 34.
5 Arno Schirokauer, in Volker Klotz, op. cit., p. 29.

Hofmannsthal's novel-fragment *Andreas* is an illustration of the presentation of a type of character contemporary in mood with that of some of Thomas Mann's earlier central figures. The young man Andreas moves from Vienna (the year is 1778) to Venice on a journey undertaken at his parents' suggestion as part of his education. He is passive in his attitudes, responsive to emotional inwardness, undemonstrative, at a loss for words though rich in thoughts and potentiality. Childhood memories of an unpleasant character are heightened by their recall in dreams. He is uncertain of the reliability he can put upon his relationship with his parents. Venice introduces him to an environment where people are quick in actions, gestures, and words, volatile and nimble, unreliable but fascinating. Andreas is confused and at times finds difficulty in distinguishing reality from appearance.

At the same time that Hofmannsthal was planning *Andreas*, Rilke was working on his *Malte Laurids Brigge* (1910). Here there are gradations from detailed realism, through borderland states of mind where the normal world breaks down, to episodes which transcend the common-sense world. The twenty-eight-year-old Malte, living alone in a depressing environment in Paris, records his impressions of the present and his memories of his lonely anxiety-ridden childhood in Denmark. Like Rilke when he was Rodin's secretary and engaged upon the *Neue Gedichte*, Malte is attempting to 'learn to see'. At times he depicts the urban scene around him with the photographic accuracy of the Naturalist, and then description becomes merged into subjective impression.

That I can't give up sleeping with the window open. Trams tear clanging through my room. Cars go over me. A door shuts. Somewhere or other a pane of glass clatters down, I hear its big pieces laugh and the little splinters giggle. Then suddenly muffled, enclosed noise from the other side, inside the house. Somebody is climbing the stairs. Coming, coming incessantly. Is here, has been here a long time, has gone past. And then the street again. A girl crows out: *Ah tais-toi, je ne veux plus*. The tram races up to this with excitement, rushes over it, away over everything. Somebody calls. People run, overtake one another. A dog barks. What a relief: a dog. Towards morning there is even a cock that crows, and that is unbounded pleasure. Then I suddenly go to sleep.

The sensations from the outside world are absorbed and transformed by the poet's imagination. There is an awareness of different and disparate layers of experience simultaneously. Malte sees a poor woman in the street, lost in her private and clearly anxious preoccupations:

The woman started and took herself out of herself, too quickly, too violently, so that her face remained in her two hands. I could see it lying there, its hollow shape. It cost me an indescribable effort to keep my attention on these hands and not to turn to look at what had torn itself away from them. I shuddered at the thought of seeing a face from the inside, but I was even more afraid of the bare, wounded, faceless head.

For the child Malte these fantasies used to assume more terrifying proportions. Groping for a pencil which he has dropped on to the carpet, he feels his hand to be something alien and uncontrollable; when a second strange hand comes from out of the wall, it is only with terror and difficulty that he can withdraw his own hand. He dresses up in front of a mirror, but becomes horrified at the unfamiliar figure staring back at him, and reflection and delusion threaten to become stronger than reality and to engulf him. The psychological realism of these experiences is expressed in terms of subjective delusion. When the supernatural intervenes, Malte can accept it without question as part of objective reality.

If Rilke's novel may be taken as an example of the fragmentation of the outside world in the poet's experience, Kafka's writing can blend the ordinary with the extraordinary in a unique and compelling way. He already takes for granted that the commonplace environment of pre-1914 Prague can combine everyday monotony with a nightmare unpredictability. In his early *Beschreibung eines Kampfes* ('Description of a Fight') he is concerned already with the instability of the common-sense world:

Do you know why I pray like that? . . . Now at last I can reveal to you why I have let myself be accosted by you. From curiosity, from hope. Your look has already comforted me a long time. And I hope to learn from you what it is about the things which sink around me like a fall of snow, while for other people even a little liqueur glass stands firm on the table like a monument.

The Expressionism of the period just before, during and after the First World War was an ecstatic radicalism which strove to combine visionary awareness with practical social purpose. In the field of fiction there is, at the periphery of the movement, the outstanding figure of Franz Kafka, through whose sketches, short stories, and three incomplete novels post-war German readers and writers have made their own discovery of symbolism in the novel, of the merging of conscious mind and dream-world, of motifs of fear, guilt, and split personality, as well as of the sense of metaphysical quest. Kafka has been interpreted in terms of religious seeking; of abnormal psychology with a Freudian basis; of social-political consciousness; or of a nihilism which expounds life as a hell guided, if there is any guidance at all, by a malevolent fiend. Then there is the thought that Kafka may be a parodist who has deliberately constructed stories that shall be open and capable of explanation in terms of any or all of such solutions. But the anguish and intense spirit of seeking that pervades his work, though so frequently accompanied by irony and humour, manifest the seriousness of Kafka's approach to his art. In his stories and novels we find no reference to contemporary events, nor to the history of civilization; there is a rigorous focusing of attention on the immediate concerns of the narrative, usually related from the point of view of one protagonist. His careful, studied, and unassuming prose is a deceptively simple-looking vehicle for the complexity of his thoughts. He expresses the probings and anxieties of the human mind stretching out with utmost effort, leaving common sense behind and venturing over the border into the irrational. The subjective seekings and fears of Kafka's artistic imagination have become compelling to general human attention.

Hermann Hesse's development as a prose-writer can be seen as illustrating a synthesis of traditional elements from the German nineteenth century with features from that writing which became known in the 1920s as marking an experimental endeavour to widen and renew the scope of the novel. His loving conservation of the mood of German Romanticism and regional realism did not prevent him from responding in his imaginative writing to myth and depth psychology (in the wake of Jung rather than of Freud), to a more radical examination of the nature of personality, and to the challenges of experiment in narrative form. Emil Sinclair, the hero of *Demian* (1919), seeks to achieve a new integration of personality in contradistinction to sterile middle-class convention. The atmosphere of Expressionist yearning for a rebirth of man and art is conveyed vividly in *Klingsors letzter Sommer* ('Klingsor's Last Summer') (1920), while *Der Steppenwolf* ('The Wolf of the Steppes') (1927) brings forward qualities of disillusionment and disharmony that emphasize the author's scepticism of a view of life that does not reckon with incursions of the chaotic. Hesse's last major work, *Das Glasperlenspiel* ('The Glass Bead Game') (1943), is set in a future time where an equable society, with its Swiss echoes, is shown as containing seeds of decay within itself. Apart from the mass of the population there exists the Castilian Order, a quasi-monastic élite which in the game of glass beads pursues a distillation of the essence of higher artistic, academic, and religious thought and experience.

The game of glass beads is thus a game with the entire contents and values of our civilization, it plays with them as a painter, for example, in the great periods of art may have played with the colours of his palette. Whatever insights, lofty thoughts and works of art mankind has produced in its creative periods, whatever subsequent epochs of learned observation have expressed in concepts and have made their intellectual possession, this huge complex of intellectual and spiritual values is played by the glass-beads player as an organ is played by an organist.

The Order is not concerned with analytical reason alone, but seeks to find the binding thread, conceived fleetingly in artistic or religious experiences, which enables the game at its best to become 'the quintessence of intellect and art, the sublime cult, the mystic union of all the separate members of the universe of letters'. In this 'sublime alchemy' the dissonances of scepticism are forbidden, and the object in view is always to be the search for harmony. Above all, music is for Hesse here the most acceptable symbol for this quest for inner unity. The practice of this cult by the intellectual élite is to act as a leaven to the society of the outside world, but the central figure, Josef Knecht, fails to find complete inner harmony, and the restlessness of the author's earlier heroes reasserts itself in his spirit. With a rarified dignity, slow-moving and somewhat remote from everyday reality, *Das Glasperlenspiel* succeeds in conjuring up an idyllic atmosphere where it is possible to unfold a universalist aspiration to apotheosize civilization's positive, ideal values.

The evocation of the largeness and dispassionate anonymity associated with twentieth-century city life is one of the features of three novels which are close to one another in time (the latter years of the Weimar Republic), in their broadness of vision wishing to extend the novel form to embrace wide facets of experience and thought, with a sober, disillusioned realism as principal mood: Alfred Döblin's *Berlin Alexanderplatz* (1929), Hermann Broch's *Die Schlafwandler* (1931–2), and Robert Musil's *Der Mann ohne Eigenschaften* (*The Man without Qualities*) (two volumes were published in 1930 and 1932; later material has been published posthumously). *Berlin Alexanderplatz* has been called a German counterpart to the work of Joyce, Dos Passos, and Jules Romains. The story of Franz Biberkopf after his release from prison, his involvement in criminal activities in the proletarian underworld of Berlin, his subsequent arrest and hospital treatment, and his final reinstatement in society as a factory porter does not demonstrate a gradual development but a rejection of an earlier personality and the assumption of a completely new one. Biberkopf's capacity to lead a life of his own is extremely limited, and he comes very close to complete disintegration; the individual cannot live in isolation, but needs the support of those around him. The central figure's thoughts are revealed directly, but authorial comment helps to underline the particular nature of his situation, while the use of montage puts him in the context of the life around him as expressed for instance through advertisements, newspaper quotations, statistical information, factual description, popular songs, and mythical-biblical analogies. Döblin gives here an essentially hopeful account of one extended episode from his hero's life, and for all the naturalistic detail his Berlin is presented with a positive vitality.

The three volumes of Broch's *Die Schlafwandler* present narratives from the years 1888, 1903, and 1918, thus allowing for a panorama with breadth in time as well as some detailed presentation of character analysis and social setting. The time-sequence allows the author to bring home his thesis concerning the 'decline of values'. Already in 1888 Prussian society is ossified and unadaptable to new developments. Church and state have a preponderant influence upon the Pasenow family, but in a largely conventional and harmful way. Bertrand, Joachim von Pasenow's more sceptical friend and mentor, looks to humane rationalism and liberalism as an ideal that is preferable to Joachim's romanticism. Esch, the representative of 'anarchy' fifteen years later, also comes into contact with Bertrand. Joachim and Esch find themselves with beliefs in common in 1918 at the time of revolutionary disturbance, though the unscrupulous 'factuality' of Huguenau triumphs. During the thirty years German, and European society as a whole, is seen as passing from the decline already present in the apparent strength of the *status quo* but only recognized consciously by a few, to an overt collapse which is seen as moral and personal as well as political. Whereas the first volume has a narrative form of traditional type, the more extended final sequence moves to the more open, experimental manner, with verse and essayistic interpolations as well as episodes involving characters whose fates have little or no direct connection with those of the central figures but none the less contribute to the general mood of the novel and place the individual character in a less central perspective.

Those parts of Musil's *Der Mann ohne Eigenschaften* which were published in 1930 and 1932 introduce a group of people, mainly from the professional classes and intelligentsia, centring upon

Vienna a little while before the outbreak of the First World War. Ulrich, the central figure, stands with ironical reserve apart from an organization, to which he acts as secretary, which is attempting unsuccessfully to find meaning and shape to a proposed 'Austrian Year' to celebrate the seventieth anniversary of the reign of Franz Josef II in 1918. This situation offers scope for extensive satire; Ulrich's dry scepticism contrasts with the enthusiasm of his cousin 'Diotima' for higher feeling and idealistic synthesis and with the florid eloquence of Arnheim, who is devoted to the cultured idealism of German classicism and to his large-scale business interests. Ulrich's attractiveness to women furnishes a number of sub-plots. The death of their father brings him into close contact with his sister Agathe after they have been apart for a considerable period; hitherto unsuspected affinities arise between them. After this interlude Ulrich returns to the more gregarious life of his Vienna circle. The narrative element, however, is frequently interrupted for the insertion of essayistic comment which is hardly an integral part of the work as a novel; the urge to provide a totality in intellectual range militates seriously against the artistic accomplishment of the work. But Ulrich's position as a 'man without qualities' is symptomatic of its time. He and his friend Walter are described as having shared a hope at the turn of the century that there might arise 'a new art, a new man, a new morality or perhaps a regrouping of society', but as having subsequently become disillusioned. If the times have been changing, they have done so in a way which arouses in Ulrich 'a universal disinclination'; 'a secret sickness has consumed the small start towards originality of genius in the earlier time'. He is without vocation and purpose, aware of the threat of fragmentation and dispersal that may lie in wait for his personality, as also for Kakanien, the state to which he belongs.

The advent of National Socialism in 1933 meant a termination, for twelve years, of free experimentation with language and narrative techniques, and of open discussion of intellectual issues that were at all likely to infringe upon the official outlook of the time. For the independent-minded author the alternatives were emigration, the withdrawal into non-committal forms of writing (such as travel-books), or waiting in silence; apart from the writers who left Germany as refugees, numerous others were forbidden to publish or else themselves chose not to publish in the course of this period. Commentators on the social scene such as Thomas and Heinrich Mann, Döblin, Broch, and Musil left the country. Their work could only become widely known again in Germany after 1945. The extent to which novelists within Germany during the war years were allowed freedom to express themselves has been discussed by H. Boeschenstein; in this context he says:

> In contrast with the style of American fiction, German diction, too often a fabric of clichés, looks faded, washed out. This condition of tepid listlessness cannot possibly be attributed to accident. . . . It is not the absence of personal linguistic virtuosity which is to be deplored, but the lack of contact with lively language. Such language is never the creation of one man only, or of a few men; it develops from a healthy emotional, intellectual, and occupational group life, from a richly integrated society that is free to air all its concerns frankly.[6]

A number of novelists who stayed in Germany then used a style that was traditional and refined, that looked back to models from earlier times (Goethe or Stifter perhaps), and that eschewed elements of the commonplace and contemporary. The form of the historical novel, in any case more popular and more highly regarded in Germany than in England, was widely employed. Personal relationships were not portrayed with realistic frankness, but could become stylized out of normality of context; Doderer's novel of Baroque Austria (*Ein Umweg*, 1940) is scarcely recognizable as the work of the author of *Die Dämonen*. It is interesting that myth and history found support not only in some novelists who remained in Germany, but also among others who left, for example in Thomas Mann's biblical tetralogy *Joseph und seine Brüder* and in his brother Heinrich's affectionate biographical novel of *Henri Quatre*, set in sixteenth-century France. Among the writers who remained in Germany were those who did express their opposition to the régime, though this had to be in veiled form.

6 H. Boeschenstein, *The German Novel, 1939–44*. Toronto, 1949, p. 3.

Introduction

There has been continuity in the German novel since 1945, in spite of the enormous sense of catastrophe and finality which that year induced. If many refugee writers did not return in person, their works did, and many writings of theirs which were newly published after 1945 directed interest to earlier phases of their output. Similarly authors of the same generation who had stayed in Germany could ensure a comparable continuity in their publications. At the same time international influences became freely available with the advent of the Allied occupation of Germany. In due course those authors who first began to publish after 1945 consolidated their reputations. The new voices too had much that was interesting to say, and a number of them have already been heard well beyond the confines of German-speaking countries.

2 'We have been forced to look around for a new basis of living. . .' (Thomas Mann)

In his essay 'Meine Zeit' (1950), Thomas Mann looked back over some of the main social-historical factors that had made their impact on him from his early years to his seventy-fifth year. It was a period that was by no means lacking in external drama, he says, and he recalls the power of Germany under Bismarck, and of Victorian Britain, while at the same time middle-class norms were being questioned and attacked; the war of 1914–18, bringing about the introduction of America into world politics and the collapse of the German Empire; the changed moral atmosphere after the war, 'the Russian Revolution; the upsurgence of Fascism in Italy and of National Socialism in Germany, the Hitler-terror, the union of East and West against it, the winning of the war and the peace that was once more lost'. Mann can compare this period with that of the Napoleonic Wars, as viewed by Goethe, and feel that the first half of the twentieth century was no less challenging and that the second half might well offer further spectacular changes in living and thinking. He sees himself and others of his generation as enjoying a considerable advantage in having known and savoured the *ancien régime* before 1914. His own life and work can thus provide a continuity, and it is in transitions rather than sudden leaps that he sees history as taking its course. With reference to the early formative years which culminated in the achievement of his first novel *Buddenbrooks* (1901), the author finds that the intellectual figures who impressed him most were Tolstoy, Wagner, and Nietzsche.

In a letter from Switzerland, of 13 March 1933, Thomas Mann explained how political developments in Germany now impelled him to remain outside his homeland, and what an abrupt change this would bring about in his personal life:

I am too good a German, too closely bound to the cultural traditions and the language of my country, for the thought of exile over years or even a lifetime not to have a hard, fateful significance for me. Yet we have been forced to look around for a new basis of living. . . . At 57 such a loss of normal existence, to which one had become accustomed and in which one was beginning to become a little stiff, may not be an insignificant matter.

For the time being the Manns settled in Switzerland, Thomas Mann's major creative writing being now devoted to *Joseph und seine Brüder* (*Joseph and his Brethren*), 1933–43, a novel of an individual's development to a yet more consistent extent than *Der Zauberberg* (*The Magic Mountain*), 1924, that other major novel in which the author could be seen as expressing a positive, indeed 'representative', attitude to the outlook of the Weimar Republic. After settling in the United States, the work of *Joseph und seine Brüder* continued, while concurrently Mann gave a lot of time and energy to the assistance of fellow-refugees and to other forms of public activity, as his letters illustrate. Contacts with France and Czechoslovakia, for instance, were kept up as long as possible, and in the United States he made repeated efforts to obtain asylum, or more favourable living conditions, for those who were exiled with him. From 1940 onwards Heinrich Mann was also living in California, at no great distance from his brother.

As he was approaching the end of *Joseph und seine Brüder* in 1942, Mann recorded the 'fun' which this task had given him. At that time he wrote about himself and his habits with humour and with a recognition of the 'bürgerlich' elements which he was again to stress in 'Meine Zeit'. He cannot accept (7 October 1941) that his life has been a hard one: 'You call my life "hard", but I cannot feel it as such. In principle I feel it gratefully as a *happy, blessed* life — I say "in principle", for it is not a question naturally of all kind of suffering, darkness and danger not being present in such a life, but of its basis being gay, so to speak sunny. . . .' His work and the preoccupation generally with art are seen here as a matter for enjoyment, not suffering: 'I am an artist, that is, someone who wishes to entertain himself—one should not put on a solemn expression about this . . . No, there can be no question of suffering in art.' It was at this time that Mann was turning over in his mind the possibility of taking up the theme of *Doktor Faustus*. Once he had begun writing this novel, the author soon became aware of the 'serious mood' it produced in him, and looked back to it soon after he had finished it (12 December 1947) as a kind of autobiography, 'a work which has cost me more and has consumed me more deeply than any earlier one'. It became one of the most discussed novels when it appeared in Germany in 1947, making a challenging impact by its use of the Faust story as a means not only of probing the problems of the artistic vocation but also of linking these problems with the role of Germany in world politics up to and including the period of the Second World War. It is the biography of a fictitious musician, but it unfolds a personality that ends in sterility and decay, not stability and maturity; the artistic temperament here is not adapted to the requirements of living in society, as was the case with Joseph, but becomes increasingly turned in upon itself. The demonic forces swamp the 'flickering flame of the spirit'. Thomas Mann no longer puts a confident case for reason and worldly wisdom, but is an impassioned, comminatory prophet. The life-story of Adrian Leverkühn allows the author to recapitulate moods and tendencies in German society as he experienced them in the years before his own exile in 1933. Born in 1885, Adrian grows up in a middle-German small-town environment which represents a link with the experience of nineteenth-century German regionalism. His theological studies allow for satire at the expense of religious institutions, both Lutheran and Catholic, which are represented by teachers who are more interested in demonology than saintliness. Adrian's choice of music as his specialization is a fatal step towards complicity with the devil. His preoccupation with musical composition is pursued persistently throughout the First World War, the period of inflation, and the most hopeful years of the Weimar Republic; his indifference to social and political issues contrasts with the attitude of his author. The group of prosperous, cultured Bohemians who are his friends in and around Munich are shown as equally remote from the problems of their time, unless they have leanings to the extreme nationalism of the Kridwiss circle. With considerable liveliness Thomas Mann reconstructs the Germany he knew, so that *Doktor Faustus* includes documented reconstruction of previous epochs of German life.

The central chapter of the novel is a dialogue with the devil in which Adrian becomes aware that he has bought the ecstasies of artistic creativity and also the depth of depression with a pact that has been signed not in blood, but in venereal infection. Modelled on Ivan's confrontation with the devil in Dostoievsky's *The Brothers Karamazov*, this scene may be regarded as a delusion of Adrian's fevered mind rather than as the consequence of a corporeal manifestation. Mann's work is almost always kept within the bounds of everyday realism, but occasionally delusion and fantasy allow for a new dimension, in this pact scene as also, for instance, in the hypnotic suggestive powers of Cipolla in *Mario und der Zauberer* (*Mario and the Magician*), 1930, a Novelle which in its criticism of Italian Fascism anticipates *Doktor Faustus*. The price Adrian has to pay for inspiration derived from pride is complete isolation: 'You may not love. . . . Your life is to be cold —therefore you may not love anyone.' By temperament Adrian is cool and undemonstrative, retreating from emotional contact with others, an uncommitted observer in all things except musical composition. But he twice tries to break the devil's bargain, when normal, simple human affection impels him to overcome the austerity of icy aestheticism. On both occasions it is a Swiss influence that kindles in him these warmer feelings. Adrian's love for Marie Godeau is shy and tentative, and his own clumsiness loses her to his friend Rudi Schwerdtfeger; disaster supervenes with Rudi's assassination in a Munich tram, and Marie feels she can have no more contact with Adrian and his circle. This somewhat novelettish episode is less impressive than Adrian's affection for his nephew Nepomuk, the child of his sister who has married a Swiss optician. Adrian develops a spontaneous fondness for the five-year-old boy, being much affected by his innocence and Swiss-German talk. His feeling for the child is much more purely affectionate than that of Aschenbach for Tadzio in *Der Tod in Venedig* (*Death in Venice*), 1913, and it is more appealing than that between Cornelius and his infant daughter in *Unordnung und frühes Leid* ('Disorder and Early Sorrow'), 1926. But Nepomuk is unpredictably stricken with cerebro-spinal meningitis, and Adrian is confronted with the problem of suffering and evil in stark terms; as he watches the child die in the midst of intense pain, he is beset by pity and indignation, like Ivan Karamazov when he too is considering the sufferings of children, and Adrian ascribes his nephew's death to the machinations of the devil. The latter chapters of the novel are told with an increasing momentum, and the reader is hurtled along at a quick pace until the catastrophe of Adrian's collapse, while he is ostensibly expounding his latest composition, 'Dr. Faustus' Lament', to his friends. If *Der Zauberberg* and *Joseph* are novels of individual development, *Doktor Faustus* might be seen as an 'Anti-Bildungsroman', a parody and reversal of the didactic optimism of this traditional German novel form.

In his treatment of the Faust theme, Mann deliberately ignores Goethe's version in order to adhere more closely to the original conception of Faust in the chap-book of 1587. Thus Thomas Mann implies a rejection of the Faustian man, and a differing interpretation from that of Goethe who in the 'Prologue in Heaven' causes the Lord to bless Faust's striving as being ultimately to a good end. Faust, the wanderer, the eagle, the amoral embodiment of sheer energy and curiosity, should be saved, as Goethe interpreted the legend; in order to make the legend apposite to his twentieth-century interpretation, Mann preferred to leave aside Goethe's approach to Faust. Adrian's life is in part based on incidents from Nietzsche's biography, such as the visit to the brothel in Leipzig, the relationship with the prostitute Esmeralda, the subsequent feverish creative activity alternating with intense depression, and the final ten years of mental collapse. In the essay 'Nietzsches Philosophie im Lichte unserer Erfahrung' ('Nietzsche's Philosophy in the Light of Contemporary Events'),

1947, Mann expresses his disagreement with Nietzsche on two issues. The latter assumed that reason was threatening to extinguish instinct, whereas, says Mann, the reverse is true, for the forces of unreason have never been more violent and dangerous than in the mid-twentieth century. If Nietzsche assumed that morality was the enemy of instinctive life, Mann asserts that the real opposites are ethics and aesthetics; it would then not be morality, but beauty that would be linked to death and destruction. While taking care to acknowledge Nietzsche's dislike of nationalism and anti-Semitism, Mann does maintain a faith in the middle-class, enlightenment values which Nietzsche attacked. As a composer, Adrian Leverkühn is faced with a sense of crisis owing to the conviction that the resources of diatonic harmony have largely been exhausted, rather on the lines of the feeling that the narrative methods of nineteenth-century realism in the novel might be threatened by as yet incalculable forms of experimentation. Adrian's music teacher, Wendell Kretschmar, expounds Beethoven's last piano sonata, which is presented as an example of a demonic German lack of formal self-control breaking through the sonata form; it is impressive, but disastrous, says Mann, and anticipates romanticism in music, the chromaticism of Wagner, and the subsequent dissolution of traditional musical harmony. 'Why must it seem to me as if almost all, in fact, all methods and devices of the art are today only still of use for purposes of parody?', Adrian asks. He becomes an atonal composer, and in order to have anything original to say musically, he is dependent on the devil's help.

Adrian is thus to contain Faust, Nietzsche, the spirit of German music, and indeed the German national character as a whole. In an essay 'Deutschland und die Deutschen' (1947), Thomas Mann develops generalizations about the association of music, the demonic and German nature which are part of the mood underlying *Doktor Faustus*: 'The Germans are people of the Romantic Counter-Revolution against the philosophical intellectualism and rationalism of the Age of Enlightenment—of a revolt of music against literature, of mysticism against clarity.'

The narrator of the novel, Dr. Serenus Zeitblom, a teacher of Classics, has been Adrian's devoted admirer and famulus from schooldays onwards. Like Settembrini in *Der Zauberberg*, he can be discursively pedagogic, but at the same time he can speak for his author. After Adrian's death in 1940, the year of Hitler's most intoxicating triumphs, Zeitblom begins collecting biographical material about his friend and writes down the life-story between May 1943 and the last days of the Third Reich two years later. Adrian's pact and decline are shown as parallel to Germany's fortunes in the course of the last two years of the war. There seems little hope at the end of *Doktor Faustus*, but there are alternatives to despair. The final high cello note of 'Dr. Faustus' Lament' is intended to bear positive significance; and even if Adrian himself is lost, Zeitblom, his other self, has survived, so that the voice of Liberal humanism may yet be heard.

Occasionally during the years when *Doktor Faustus* was a major preoccupation, Mann was reminded that *Buddenbrooks* and *Tonio Kröger* still possessed an appeal to many readers that his later writings did not. He was resigned about this, though with the completion of *Doktor Faustus* he did wonder whether perhaps this was not a work which would equal his earlier ones in immediate interest and emotional response. With the publication of *Doktor Faustus* a phase of his life was virtually completed: 'After *Faustus* I can no longer take anything really seriously. "That will not come again", Fontane said after *Effi Briest*.' (10 September 1949). Seeing himself as a late-comer who was rounding off an era that was almost past, he could welcome Philip Toynbee's description of him as 'the lonely world-citizen'. His three last works of fiction all aroused his misgivings as he was working on them. *Der Erwählte* ('The Chosen One', English translation published as *The Holy Sinner*),[1] 1951, retells a medieval legend with the embellishment of irony and linguistic jokes; the juxtaposition of American English and Middle High German may be intended to suggest the cosmopolitan nature of modern literature as being parodistically

1 English titles printed in italics are the titles of published English translations. English titles printed in roman type are direct renderings of the German.

comparable to the internationalism of medieval Christendom. Gregory, born in incest, grows up to marry his mother, then repents for seventeen years of self-imposed asceticism, until he is elevated to the Papacy, so that his wife-and-mother comes now to venerate him as 'father'. At the time he was engaged on his work, Mann was expressing in his correspondence various misgivings about events and ideas that were current in Germany, including his mistrust of the policies of Adenauer. He was, however, also to tell correspondents more than once that the treatment of the themes of sin and grace in *Der Erwählte* is serious.

The setting of the Novelle *Die Betrogene* ('The Deceived Woman', English translation published as *The Black Swan*), 1953, is the period after the First World War. Rosalie von Tümmler embodies a mixture of self-discipline, snobbery, and easy emotionalism; she is a 'great friend of nature'. What she fancies as a reawakening to 'life' reveals itself as the advent of death in the shape of a haemorrhage precipitated by cancer of the womb. She is temporarily transmuted by flirtation with a vigorous, careless young American in the figure of Ken Keaton; but this miracle of restoration is shortlived and only anticipates a complete and humiliating collapse. This clinical taste may well be a further afterthought of the author's on the German political situation. *Felix Krull* (1954), 'The confessions of a confidence-trickster', attained an immediate popularity among German readers of the time which was gratifying to the author in the last year of his life, particularly as the immediately preceding works had been a source of controversy. This light, carefree comedy was begun much earlier in the author's career, at the time of *Der Tod in Venedig* and *Königliche Hoheit* ('Royal Highness'), and it is remarkable how Thomas Mann in his old age was able to recapture the deftness and agility of forty years earlier. Felix Krull narrates his own story from the standpoint of enforced leisure presented by a prison sentence; the work is, however, a fragment, and its action does not present events leading directly up to a conclusion. The rogue-hero is in the first place a device for unfolding a series of episodic adventures, and it is not to be expected that he should develop, but rather that he should come through his experiences unscathed and unchanged. Whereas the hero of a *Bildungsroman* may be earnest, idealistic, and dependent upon the guidance of others, like Wilhelm Meister or Hans Castorp, the picaresque hero lives by his wits and is untroubled by scruples. Felix's family background is not the North German milieu of Hans Castorp or Tonio Kröger, but that of the wine-growing Rhineland. With some analogies with Joseph, Felix exploits his artistic temperament and social adaptability. He leaves Germany to find a more congenial jumping-off ground for his adventures in Paris. As a waiter in a hotel he has opportunities to marry a young woman from Birmingham and to accompany an older man to aristocratic solitude in the Highlands, but he resists these opportunities and is rewarded by the more exciting offer of proceeding to Portugal under an assumed noble identity. It is not until the journey to the south begins that the full picaresque machinery is set in motion and Felix enters the 'great world'. Situations which in previous works had been treated with seriousness are here presented without sinister implications as sheer entertainment. The happiest moment in his life, Felix decides, as he looks back during his time in prison, was the afternoon when at the age of eight he was provided with a toy violin and extravagant clothes and allowed to mimic in public the performance of a Hungarian dance by a member of a café orchestra. 'Music enchants me, indeed, although I have never taken the opportunity of learning to perform, this dreamy art possesses in me a fanatical adorer. . . .' Felix is a less scrupulous Joseph to whom Paris in the 1890s opens up a new life comparable to the Egypt of the Pharaohs.

Mann's last three fictional works were not written with the ardent belief in a mission such as underlay the work on *Doktor Faustus*. He wrote to his daughter Erika (7 June 1954): 'I must often think that it would have been better if I had taken my leave of this world after *Faustus*.' But he went on to outline further plans for the future, emphasizing the necessity for him to have work and active hope. For such late work he would see humour as a major ingredient, and entertainment as a prime intention; yet this aim can take on other worldly aspects: 'It was always my wish and purpose to entertain, but would one take so much trouble about it if it were only directed at human beings? Art, it is said, aims at perfection. But that is in fact not so entirely earthly an endeavour.' Thomas Mann has commanded attention from the beginning of this century onwards, both as teacher and entertainer, and his eminence as a leading novelist of his time is firmly established. The vigour and commitment of his personality remained with him to the end of his life.

His elder brother Heinrich Mann (1871–1950) clearly shared many experiences with the more widely celebrated Thomas. Already before the First World War Heinrich Mann had become an admirer of the French tradition of rationalism and liberalism, and after 1914 the brothers were estranged for some years on account of their differing loyalties during that period. They came together in their support for the Weimar Republic, and both left Germany in 1933. Shortly before the beginning of the Second World War Heinrich Mann lived in France, an important literary product of this time being the extended biographical novel *Henri Quatre* (1935–38), a mellow tribute to the French king who is seen as an embodiment of humane values. The two novels of Heinrich Mann which appeared after 1945, while he was resident in the United States, also have French associations, though neither work is as satisfying as *Henri Quatre. Der Atem* ('Breath'), 1949, centres upon the mysterious figure of Lydia Kowalski, in particular upon the last hours of her life which coincide with the outbreak of war in 1939; the scene is Nice and its neighbourhood. Lydia was once a great lady, but her husband took his life in May 1914 and her lover Fernand deserted her and left her impoverished. She has been a factory-worker since, but now pays a daily visit to a Nice bank in the forlorn expectation that money will be there for her. On the morning of this particular day her breathing is difficult and she more than once collapses; but a series of adventures befall her, linking her fate with political intrigues and clashes between representatives of industrialism and proletariat, while at the same time she receives the affection and respect of simple people, who see her as one of themselves and yet also as a great lady from another era and place. In a sequence of happenings that is unexpected, she moves from street to bank and bank-manager's flat, from hotel bedroom to gambling casino, and from night-club to the death-bed scenes at the hotel. A fortune is won, but it can have little meaning for her now. The novel proliferates into various subsidiary actions, and contains much that is bizarre, though the heroine is presented as having a grandeur that transcends the limitations and follies of her surroundings. *Empfang bei der Welt* ('Reception for the World'), 1956, devotes its main, central section to the description of a fashionable reception, attended largely by wealthy business-men and by people from the world of opera. It has been organized by Arthur, an opera agent, who hopes to raise funds for the establishment of an opera-house. The earlier mood of the assembly, one of self-absorbed hardness, yields to an interlude of relaxed amiability before most of the guests disperse; the final stages of the party, for the few that remain, contain elements of the gross and grotesque. It is a cosmopolitan atmosphere, with snatches of dialogue in French and other languages. Although the grotesque elements have at times a threatening quality, the satire is resolved into a fairy-tale idyllic finale. Arthur's father Balthasar dies at the age of ninety in his wine-cellar where he keeps his hidden hoard of gold: '"The first time that I really enjoyed my life was when I could play the poor man and hide my gold."' The old man's fate and testament bring the young couple, Arthur's son André and Stephanie, to a full realization of their love for each other. They propose to reject the fortune bequeathed to them and to transfer it to Melusine, Stephanie's mother and a bank director, and to Arthur, who have likewise confirmed their affection for one another after the reception. If those who are older feel an emotional need for money and complicated living, the young lovers can tolerate, even sympathize with this need, without sharing it.

In 1933 Alfred Döblin (1878–1957) left Germany and shortly afterwards settled in France, though with the German occupation of France in 1940 he moved again, this time to the United States; he came back to Germany for a time after the end of the war, with an official position in the French Zone. During his years of exile from Germany Döblin was working on the novel *November 1918*, which was completed in 1943 and published in 1948-50. The action of this work is centred on the events of the winter 1918-19, concentrating principally on the stormy days of the revolution in Berlin. Döblin clearly has no regrets here for the passing of the old pre-war civilization, and the hero of his work is the revolution itself rather than any of the individuals partici-pating in it. The president, Ebert, and the leader of the Freikorps, Noske, are shown in a poor light by comparison with the Sparta-cist leaders Rosa Luxemburg and Karl Liebknecht, whom the author wishes to vindicate. The narration of these public political events is less satisfying than the action which describes the attempt of an ex-army officer to return to his pre-war occupation as a schoolmaster, his conversion to the Spartacist cause and his subsequent years of anonymous pilgrimage. This novel is com-parable to Jules Romains's *Les Hommes de bonne volonté* or John Dos Passos's *U.S.A.* in the attempt to present the wide range of a large city by means of a series of parallel actions which are linked mainly by the context of their time and place. In spite of many gripping incidents the work is hardly convincing as a whole, and is less compelling than *Berlin Alexanderplatz*. Döblin's last novel *Hamlet oder Die lange Nacht nimmt ein Ende* ('Hamlet, or The Long Night Comes to an End'), written 1945-6, and published 1956, has as its initial theme the homecoming of a young man after severe injury of body and mind in the war; the centre of narrative interest, however, moves from Edward to his parents Gordon and Alice Allison. The setting is for the most part a family house in the English countryside and it is predominantly an English cultural environment which is presented to the reader. In its form the work is reminiscent of Boccaccio's *Decameron* or Goethe's *Unterhaltungen deutscher Ausgewanderten* ('Entertainments of German Emigrés'); at a time of crisis and uncertainty a group of people agree to present stories orally to each other. The father, a professional writer, makes the suggestion, and their medical adviser hopes that the entertainment will act as a form of therapy. In this respect some success is achieved, since with the passing of the novel's time Edward is restored to balance and well-being; but with his recovery comes the collapse of his parents' relationship to one another, indeed the breakdown of their stability. The possessive mother is particularly vulnerable, but so too is Gordon, the father whose good intentions have been much misunderstood. The inset-stories have implications for the issues at stake in the main narrative; at the same time they provide points of reference to archetypal prefigurations, as in the stories of Pluto and Persephone, of Theodora, of the troubadour Jaufie, and of Lear. Edward's uncle, James Mackenzie, at one point sees Edward as going the way of a Hamlet 'to whom the task of action was given not by the ghost of a dead father, but by his own morbid inner impulse, just as are imagination and empirical experience'; Gordon Allison says: 'To have imagination means to experience complete reality.'

The search for totality of experience had been expressed by Hermann Broch (1886–1951) mainly on the social plane in the trilogy *Die Schlafwandler* (*The Sleepwalkers*), 1931–2. He wrote an essay 'James Joyce und die Gegenwart' ('James Joyce and the Present'), 1936, in honour of Joyce's birthday, and in the epilogue to *Die Schuldlosen* ('The Innocent Ones'), 1950, he endowed Leopold Bloom with a representative significance extending well beyond the confines of *Ulysses*. In this epilogue Broch has indicated something of his approach to fiction, summing up what he considered to be the function of the novel. The novel, he says, must depict a 'world totality', increasingly difficult though this is as the world becomes more complex and incoherent. This totality must not be on one plane only, since the novelist need not be limited by the naturalist convention, but should include the moral and metaphysical. Can the novel have a social purpose, he asks. Only the converted will be convinced, scepticism may say; but nevertheless the purpose of art is to be moral—it is to be 'Läuterung', purification, and Broch cites Goethe's *Faust*.

Der Tod des Vergil (*The Death of Virgil*), 1945, took shape as a short story in 1937; the author left Austria in 1938 and lived subsequently in the United States, where this material was developed into a novel. This record of the last eighteen hours of Virgil's life is a vast interior monologue that reflects the sensations and thoughts of a highly sensitive and intelligent man who knows that he is dying; the monologue is only interrupted by conversation that the poet himself hears or takes part in. The work covers a whole range of experience, from the crudity of the drunken revellers in the street outside to the most abstract expressions of the poet's quest for truth; it carries within it a wide historical synthesis, and Broch himself has said that the parallels between the first pre-Christian century and his own time are deliberate. On his death-bed the poet wants to destroy the manuscript of his *Aeneid*; art is not enough, and moreover his has been an art that has allowed itself to be subordinated to ends that he now considers unworthy. In his last hours Virgil sees his own life and its problems in a new light. There is a highly wrought scene between the emperor Augustus and the poet which brings the human issues of the work to a dramatic climax, the outcome of which is Virgil's presentation of his epic as a gift to Augustus from motives of loving self-sacrifice.

For all Broch's conscious affinities to James Joyce in his experimental technique, there is an important difference between their approaches. Broch's writing expresses firm ethical beliefs which separate him from Joyce's outlook, as expressed in Stephen Dedalus's 'I will not serve'. There is nothing parodistic in the Salvation Army scenes or in Esch's Bible study in *Die Schlafwandler*; *Die unbekannte Größe* (*The Unknown Quantity*), 1933, preaches the futility of the search for knowledge if this is divorced from the developed heart. The didactic element is present too in *Die Schuldlosen*, with its castigation of indifference and of refusal to assume moral and political responsibility. *Die Schuldlosen* is an interesting, if uneven experiment. The author has taken a number of his early sketches and tales, written in the first place independently of each other, and has added to them new stories with the aim, imperfectly realized, of bringing the whole into one coherent narrative. This 'novel in eleven stories' is a series of tales which can be taken as separate works, but which are also to be read as consecutive sections of a whole work. Like *Die Schlaf-wandler* it covers three periods of time, 1913, 1923, and 1933, as the earlier novel had its three sections, 1888, 1903, and 1918. Behind the surface reality of the middle-class sphere in which the action is unfolded there looms a complex scaffolding of symbolism.

Broch's *Der Versucher* ('The Tempter'), as edited and published after the author's death by Felix Stössinger in 1953, is on the broad scale of *Die Schlafwandler* and *Der Tod des Vergil*. It is set in an Austrian Alpine community, and its action may be assumed to take place during the period when Broch was first working on it, the years 1934–6. It is interesting that after *Der Tod des Vergil* and *Die Schuldlosen* Broch went on to make more use of traditional narrative methods, and this last novel shows clearly his control over action, suspense, and characters conceived in these terms. A remote and largely primitive village populace succumbs to the oratory of a vagrant fanatic; in a wave of mass hysteria this man's influence reaches its height in the committing of a ritual murder. The action is seen through the eyes of the village doctor, a middle-aged man who has forsaken eminence in the city for the obscurity of general practice in this out-of-the-way spot; he is a complex figure, one of the community of rough peasants and their familiar confidant, and yet separated from them by his work and background. As a three-dimensional novel of village life *Der Versucher* has something of the vitality and grandeur of Jeremias Gotthelf's narratives of Bernese country life—in particular the theme of healing recalls the issues of the Swiss author's *Anne Bäbi Jowäger*; however, Gotthelf's peasant families have a norm of Christian belief which is lacking here, for the weakness of the Church's influence in this village is one of the factors which permit the tempter to lead it astray. Broch combines straightforward narrative with visions and monologues indicative of primitive, tellurian forces. His protagonist says:

Our life is dreaming and waking at once, and if the chill wind of dreams occasionally blows into that world which we call reality—and it does so more often than we think—this reality becomes sometimes strangely illuminated and deep like a landscape after a cool shower of rain, or like speech which all at once is no longer a mere string of words telling of things that have happened in some shapeless limbo, but which has been breathed upon by a higher reality and has suddenly gained the power to portray things as they are with life and warmth.

The rhapsodic evocation of subconscious perspectives of symbolic depth does not wholly blend with the straightforward depiction of people and action in terms of common-sense realism. The different layers of perception remain disparate, so that the problem of combining them in an artistic whole is still unsolved. This last novel of Broch's is nevertheless fascinating and powerful.

Franz Werfel (1890–1945) turned to novel writing after making his name in the vanguard of the Expressionist movement primarily with verse and drama. He left Austria for France in 1938, and from there went to the United States. Religious themes had already played some part in his work before the success of *Das Lied von Bernadette* (*The Song of Bernadette*), 1941, made this story of the healing at Lourdes a best-seller. His last novel was a vision of life 100,000 years ahead, *Sternder Ungeborenen* ('Star of the Unborn'), 1946. Its picture of the future is more circumstantial than that of Hesse's *Das Glasperlenspiel*, though less poetic and refined in style. Werfel speculates freely on the details of possible intellectual and technical developments, such as inter-planetary travel. In its Californian background, its spiritualistic framework, and its general approach to intellectual problems, *Stern der Ungeborenen* has something of Aldous Huxley's *Time Must Have a Stop* and the earlier *Brave New World*. The author portrays a world-state which has been in existence in its present highly developed and comfortable way for many centuries. Life is longer, but the world population is smaller, and each individual is more precious and more delicate. This civilization, with its abundance of amenities, is, however, threatened with collapse through the extension of the 'jungle' reservations, tracts of land inhabited by primitives of a twentieth-century type. The 'astromental' world is finally over-run by the jungle dwellers, and for the most part its inhabitants choose suicide when faced by this situation. Werfel's portrayal of an over-refined civilization that collapses before a new assertion of instinctive vitality is undoubtedly compelling.

Carl Zuckmayer (born 1896) although more widely known as a dramatist, has been writing prose fiction as well as plays since the 1920s. He had to give up the home of his choice near Salzburg in 1938, and spent the war years in the United States. The vitality and down-to-earth humour which Zuckmayer has at his disposal is revealed in the tale *Der Seelenbräu* (1945), which gives a picture of incidents from life in an Austrian village community. The local priest is jocularly known as 'Seelenbräu(tigam)', 'bridegroom of the soul', on account of his rendering of a popular item of religious music; his counterpart and rival in the neighbourhood is the village publican, a personality representing in particular the pleasures of food and drink. *Die Fastnachtsbeichte* (*Carnival Confession*), 1959, is written in a mood of sombre seriousness, where the starkness of the action contrasts with the apparent gaiety of the setting, Carnival time in 1913 in Mainz, a city which was closely associated with the author's youthful background. It is a story of the uneasy relationship between past guilt and the seeming stability of the present. Adelbert Panezza, 'Carnival Prince' for the time being, is a prosperous owner of a saw-mill, a brick factory, and a vineyard in a village near Mainz. The shortcomings of his earlier life, especially in his attitude to his illegitimate son, are issues that he has to contend with again after the son's return to Mainz and his murder on Carnival-Saturday. Guilt is, however, by no means limited to one central figure, and the author's skilful exposition maintains tension throughout. The restless movements of masked revellers emphasize further the problems of dissociating appearance and reality.

Oskar Maria Graf (1894–1967) published in *Unruhe um einen Friedfertigen* ('Unrest about a Peaceable Man'), 1947, a novel centring upon a Bavarian country community during the period extending from shortly before the First World War until 1933.

The 'peaceable man' is a shoemaker who comes with wife and one son to settle in a village where he hopes to be able to make his living in peace. His wife's death and his son's precipitate emigration to America confirm his desire to avoid involvement in any of the private or public events that take place around him. The rural locality is, however, shown as affected by the political and economic issues of the day, from the deprivations of war-time to the uncertainties of the revolutionary period in Bavaria after 1918, from the interlude of the inflation, when the farmers enjoy unprecedented but often unstable prosperity, to the first months of 1933. If the shoemaker Kraus is for the most part an onlooker, two younger men become leading figures and enemies in the political conflicts that flare up intermittently, but dangerously, in the area. Silvan, the Nazi, can triumph in 1933, while Ludwig, a Left Wing supporter, escapes to Austria after great difficulties, and subsequently to America. Although considerable stress is laid on the political issues, there is careful and loving portrayal of village life, with a varied gallery of figures that are characterized with robust vigour.

Graf's 'novel of a future', *Die Eroberung einer Welt* ('The Conquest of a World'), 1948, was written in America before the end of the Second World War. The story envisages a chaotic situation at the conclusion of the Third World War which is eventually resolved by the establishment of a humane world government. His 'New York novel', *Die Flucht ins Mittelmäßige* ('Flight into the Mediocre'), 1959, directs attention to a group of German-speaking expatriates living in New York in the post-war period and to some of the problems of living as part of this 'diaspora'. Martin Ling, a widower in his late fifties, is the central figure. Episodes from his earlier years in Germany and, as a refugee, in Czechoslovakia are recalled, while further inset material is provided by the stories which Ling recounts at the social evenings of the Kumians. Eventually persuaded to start writing stories for publication, Ling finds success, and therewith a problematic transformation of his personality. His relationship with another writer who has gained popularity is compared, by one of his friends, to that of Faust with Mephistopheles. Within a fairly short time Ling finds himself estranged from many of those he previously knew, and after catastrophes befalling those around him, for some of which he feels accountable, he gives up writing, declaring: 'I want to live like anyone else, like one of the crowd. Simply to live and to be ordinary, nothing else, nothing at all!' This novel is a sympathetic and graphic presentation of some aspects of middle age, depicting the stresses of living and of being urged to creativity in an environment that in the last resort is not home. Martin Ling, like Ludwig in *Unruhe um einen Friedfertigen* after his emigration to the United States, has suffered from his forcible uprooting from the environment of his earlier life, 'a man between the past and the uncomprehended present.'

Hermann Kesten's *Die Zwillinge von Nürnberg* ('The Twins of Nürnberg'), 1947, combines comedy with political satire. It follows the chief public events and moods of the two periods described, the two years after the end of the First World War and the years 1938–45. Everything that happens in the complicated but neatly contrived plot is within the bounds of reason, but only just. The twins Primula and Uli get married, the former to an ex-officer who later becomes an official in Goebbels's ministry, the latter to a writer who has to emigrate to Paris because of his humanitarian ideals. Primula becomes the mother of twin boys, both of whom later turn against the Nazi outlook. The last chapters, depicting both the life of German emigrants in Paris and the conditions in Germany shortly before the outbreak of war in 1939, are more serious in tone than the earlier part of the book. The final chapter shows with great effect the confrontation of Primula, still loyal to the outlook of wartime Germany, with her son Alexander, now a lieutenant in the American army, over the ruins of Nürnberg in 1945. This novel excels in the skill of its management of plot and dialogue. *Die fremden Götter* ('The Strange Gods'), 1949, takes as its main theme the conflict between a father and his daughter over religious loyalties. Schott has become a firm believer in the orthodox Jewish faith of his fathers, but Luise has accepted the Roman Catholic faith taught her in the convent where she was looked after during those war years when her parents were in a concentration camp. The setting is the south of France. After a series of comedy-style adventures Luise is to marry the young man of her choice, though her father is by no means reconciled to this situation.

Im Westen nichts Neues ('Nothing New in the West', English translation published as *All Quiet On the Western Front*), 1929, established the popular reputation of Erich Maria Remarque (1898–1970) and became one of the most widely read novels about the First World War. His *Arc de Triomphe* (1946), the story of a German refugee surgeon in Paris just before the last war, has been a best-seller too. In *Der Himmel hat keine Günstlinge* (*Heaven Has No Favourites*), 1961, Remarque writes a love-story concerning a motor racing-driver and a sufferer from tuberculosis; backgrounds in Switzerland, France, and Italy are lightly and efficiently sketched in. *Die Nacht von Lissabon* (*The Night in Lisbon*), 1962, is a sympathetic evocation of the plight of German refugees from National Socialism. A man who calls himself Schwarz decides to give his long sought-after permit to emigrate from Europe to America to a fellow refugee in Lisbon. In the course of a night in 1942 he explains his reasons to the latter and thereby unfolds the story of his adventures between Germany and France after 1933, his internment in September 1939 and his flight southwards after the German occupation of France had begun.

Theodor Plievier (1892–1955) completed shortly before his death a trilogy which is a large-scale epic of the war between Germany and Russia and its aftermath. His manner of composition hardly applies to fiction in the normal sense, for there is so much emphasis on documentation and the narration of tactical movements that few of the many characters receive individual treatment. This is particularly the case with the first two volumes of the work. *Stalingrad* (1945) surveys the events leading to the defeat of the Germans in Stalingrad in January 1943. Its sequel *Moskau* (1952) takes as its starting-point the first days of the German invasion of Russia in 1941, and culminates in the approach of the fateful Russian winter as the Germans stand before Moscow.

Plievier had unique facilities for collecting the material for his work; as a refugee from Germany in 1933, he made his way to Russia, and was allowed to observe the scene and sift documents of this piece of history. The events of the war in the east are told as a vivid and detailed piece of reporting in the naturalist manner. The impetus behind Plievier's writing turns from political theory to a more universal sympathy and pity. In *Moskau* a German whose life has been spared by Russian partisans reflects:

'Germans and Russians lay frozen in the snow.
'What had they wanted? What had their rulers intended with them? They wanted to decide the fate of Europe. Not for the first time. . . . Charles XII was ruined on the fields of Poltava. The French musketeers of Napoleon failed. The German grenadiers now lay on the same frozen earth. Europe remained unborn, and the peoples on either side of the bloody wound are suffering hopelessly. . . .'

The words of an old Russian man offer prophetic meaning to the despairing German: '"The earth has been given to men from God's hands without any frontiers. . . . The whole earth belongs to all, entirely!"' *Berlin* (1954), the longest of the three parts of the work, brings the novel to its conclusion. As an imaginative work it is the most satisfactory part of the whole, for Plievier brings to life the city of Berlin and the surrounding Eastern Zone with a vigour and variety of treatment that make fascinating reading. There is much that must be autobiographical in this novel which traces the fortunes of Berlin from the last days of Hitler in April 1945 through the early days of Russian occupation until it concludes with the abortive rising of June 1953; after holding an official post in the East, Plievier went to the West in 1947. There is an impressive picture of Berlin burning and of Hitler's final phase, before the narrative moves on to showing for the most part the struggles of a politician who tries to administer just government in the Eastern Zone, and the life of German prisoners of war in Russian hands.

The major work of Hans Henny Jahnn (1894–1959) is the novel *Fluß ohne Ufer* ('River without Banks') which he was writing during his exile on Bornholm from 1933 onwards. The title indicates the theme: the river of life, or the stream of consciousness, which is a demonic, elemental force knowing no control. Jahnn's hero learns to identify himself with the raw, teeming life of sailors' quarters in South American and African ports and the bleaker poverty of a Norwegian coastal community. Gustav Anias Horn loses his fiancée when the *Lais*, a ship with a mysterious freight, goes down, and the memory of this catastrophe throws his whole life out of course. He refuses to see his parents again or to assume normal social responsibilities, but in perverse friendship with the man who murdered his fiancée lives first among half-castes and negroes and later in isolation in Scandinavia. A rebel against all traditional usages, he is passionately indignant at the injustice of race and class distinctions. A cultured handful of white folk in America and Europe may be in fact the conscious mind of humanity, but let them beware of their dependence on the inarticulate but vast and vital mass of mankind who are beneath them. If materialism is taken to be the right interpretation of the world, all life is equally holy, and if all life is holy, then life's fulfilment in the present should not be distorted by the memory of past failures. It is the paradox of Horn's life that as a man of forty-nine he is haunted by the shadows of a catastrophe that befell the ship *Lais* twenty-seven years before, although he has so strenuously been trying to live for the moment and to deny the validity of any code that would compel him to assume a responsibility which he resents. *Fluß ohne Ufer* is, like Mann's *Doktor Faustus* and Broch's *Der Tod des Vergil*, in part a 'Künstlerroman', a novel about an artist. Horn gradually realizes his potentialities as a musician and composer (Jahnn refers in an essay 'Über den Anlaß' ('Concerning the Cause'), 1954, to his admiration for the Danish composer Carl Nielsen). Characteristically enough, it is a pianola in a seedy South American hotel that makes the young man thrill to the discovery of a new talent. This work has eruptive violence and nightmarish qualities. Horn preserves the body of his dead friend and keeps the coffin as a piece of house-furniture. After his murder at the hands of Ajax von Uchri, the latter assumes the identity of Horn's dead friend Tutein and enters into a relationship with Horn's adolescent son Nikolaj, who has been brought up in the family of the horsedealer Egil Bohn. The *Epilog* (1961), edited by Walter Muschg after the author's death, is not completed, but is a substantial narrative of events taking place in the months following the murder of Horn. The boy Nikolaj becomes confirmed in his musical vocation, while Ajax von Uchri develops a concern for the boy's development. In the *Epilog* Jahnn brings forward a number of episodes centring upon more peripheral figures: the relationship of Gemma Bohn to her children, Xavier Faltin's organization of the memorial concert of Horn's music and his subsequent illness and death, Faltin's children, and the adolescent development of Nikolaj's half-brothers Asger and Sverre.

The incident at the opening of the second book of *Die Niederschrift des Gustav Anias Horn* ('The Account of Gustav Anias Horn') is indicative of one recurrent set of motifs in Jahnn's work and in part of his manner:

I was deeply stirred. I will relate it briefly: I heard out of a heap of loosely piled-up dry pine twigs the beating of the wings of a big insect. I came close and recognized a dragon-fly which was fluttering anxiously in the open lattice-work of the small branches. It was not possible to recognize at once why the creature did not seek freedom, which seemed so easy to attain. It pushed against the ground with its head. It did not seem to recognize its surroundings. I bent down and now saw that a number of ants were spraying acid over the dragon-fly's great netted eyes; others were biting with their mandibles into those very eyes. I quickly stepped in to liberate the creature. It was too late. It had already been blinded, or partially blinded. It fell, beating its wings, to earth. . . . It died within a minute of over-strain, having succumbed to a heart-attack or to the unimaginable pain of blinding.

The maiming and destruction of the good and beautiful is seen as something horrifying but inevitable. In the *Epilog* Faltin's son Frode, a biologist, is haunted by the cruelty and destruction which he sees as built into natural life; if nature has no place for pity, 'the awareness and acknowledgement of the pain of others', man can develop this quality. Lyrical moods and idyllic moments frequently appear as part of the texture of Jahnn's style, as well as other incidents of stark ferocity.

The short novel *Die Nacht aus Blei* ('The Night of Lead'), 1956, is a terse, closely woven piece of writing that is dominated by an atmosphere of the incalculable and apparently inevitable, concentrated within a few hours of a night in an unknown city that becomes increasingly solitary and dark. The protagonist Matthieu fails to make contact with whatever may lie behind the one illuminated window he first sees. He is reluctant to make advances to Franz and Elvira, while his subsequent meeting with Andreas ('Anders', his double at an earlier time of life) leads finally to his witnessing the latter's death in his underground cellar, when the last light, a flickering candle, goes out. In utter darkness and knowing no way out of the enclosing cellar, Matthieu nevertheless senses the returning presence of the 'dark angel' who had left him at the beginning of the story. With few requisites here, Jahnn has given compelling shape to a vision of life and death.

3 '. . . After all there may still be a hope.' (Ernst Jünger)

WERNER BERGENGRUEN (1892–1964) describes in his auto-biographical *Schreibtischerinnerungen* ('Writing Desk Memories'), 1961, his impressions of living and writing in Germany during the period of National Socialist domination. It was a time when this author could live as normally as any German could then and could work at his writing without outward hindrance. He was able to be concerned with personal cares and to give much thought and energy to imaginative work; indeed the two novels he published during that period are almost certainly his most memorable achievement in the genre. Bergengruen describes how none the less private worries were for twelve years persistently overshadowed by an overwhelming preoccupation with the public events precipitated by the régime of that time.

One suffered with all who were persecuted, deported, tortured and murdered. One was fearful for friends and those of like mind. One had to advise and help, without considering how lacking in advice and help one often felt personally. One had to maintain forcibly in oneself and in others the hope which repeatedly gave the appearance of fore-saking one definitely.

However, we got through that period, astonishing and incredible as this seemed afterwards.

Bergengruen put a conscious stress on action and dramatic con-struction in his writing, increasingly so as his work progressed. *Das große Alkahest* ('The Great Alkahest'), 1926, is not as yet written in the incisive, economic style of the author's last work, but it contains themes which recur frequently there. The incom-patibility of true religion with worldly power and the constant tension between ruler and ruled are brought out in the relation-ship of the arbitrary father von Karp and his timid and irresponsible son who leaves Poland for St. Petersburg. *Der Großtyrann und das Gericht* ('The Tyrant and Judgement', English translation published as *A Matter of Conscience*), 1935, deservedly one of the most widely read novels of its time in Germany, brings out Bergengruen's concern for morality and judgement in a vigorously dramatic manner; psychological analysis and descriptive atmosphere are reduced to a minimum, so that the action may be revealed in a series of conversations; the culprit, who is ruler of a small Italian Renaissance state, exposes by his action the demoralizing and confusing results of his particular form of subordinating principle to expediency. It is both an allegory and a detective story of great competence. *Am Himmel wie auf Erden* ('On Earth as It Is in Heaven'), 1940, is set in Berlin in the early sixteenth century. Although the events of the six weeks involved are complex, the whole is convincing, and the historical background is carefully filled in. The main theme is fear; Carion, astrologer to the Elector Joachim, foresees a new Flood of biblical proportions that will destroy Berlin. The Elector tries to prevent panic by suppressing the prophecy, while at the same time wishing to act upon it. The flood, of course, does not materialize; but this fear is replaced in Carion's case by a greater terror—the anticipation of leprosy. In *Schreibtischerinnerungen* Bergengruen describes the origins and genesis of these two novels, indicating their relevance to events in Germany of the time, and arguing his case for the historical novel as a valid and challenging prose medium.

It was to be expected that a writer of Bergengruen's gifts should turn to the Novelle, and probably such polished short works as *Die drei Falken* ('The Three Falcons'), 1937, *Der spanische Rosenstock* ('The Spanish Rose-tree'), 1941, and *Das Beichtsiegel* ('The Seal of the Confession'), 1946, have been more widely read than the novels. The collection of tales *Der Tod von Reval* ('Death in Reval'), 1939, treats the theme of death, but with a macabre humour that is far removed from the mood of *Die drei Falken* or *Das Beichtsiegel*. Bergengruen has written a study of E. T. A. Hoffmann, and these tales which look back to the legends and gossip of the Baltic seaboard where the author spent his early years are worthy representatives of the tradition of fantasy and realism peculiar to Hoffmann's work. The volume *Sternenstand* ('The Position of the Stars'), 1947, contains brief stories of often anecdotal character, set in the Italian Renaissance. Two subsequent collections of stories are rather more substantial than *Sternenstand*. *Die Flamme im Säulenholz* ('The Flame in the Timber Beam'), 1955, brings back the author's memories of the Baltic lands, dominated by a nostalgia for earlier times. *Zorn, Zeit und Ewigkeit* ('Anger, Time and Eternity'), 1959, contains stories which show the involvement of the natural and the supernatural, the whole being enveloped in a faith in divine providence; the story which gives the volume its title is impressive in its linking of early associations with later distress and in its clarification of a troubled state of mind.

Bergengruen's writing after 1945 did not take up again the formal challenge of a tightly-knit large-scale structure as in *Am Himmel wie auf Erden*. *Pelageja* (1947) is a short novel, a tale of shipwreck and adventure in North America in the early nineteenth century. Related by a sailor who has survived the experience, the story is not only simple in its narrative method, but is so straightforward in its approach to the human problem that the reader feels himself in a world of boyhood adventure, and one that is less complex than that of Robert Louis Stevenson's *Treasure Island*. *Das Feuerzeichen* ('The Beacon'), 1949, has as hero a man who recalls Kleist's Michael Kohlhaas; living on the Baltic coast at the beginning of the present century, this man bitterly resents an injustice and the assumed slight on his sense of honour, and finally commits suicide. This novel is close to *Der Großtyrann und das Gericht* in theme, though perhaps less fresh and absorbing. *Der letzte Rittmeister*, (*The Last Captain of Horse*), 1952, is a work with an atmosphere all of its own, a quaint exoticism spiced with playful irony. The book is dominated by the mellow personality of an old ex-captain of horse who grew up in the army traditions of Tsarist Russia and after 1918 drifted about Europe in resigned and by no means unhappy obscurity until he settled to spend his last years in the Tessine. The author, writing as a friend of his old age, records twenty-four short tales which he has heard from the Rittmeister's lips. Many of these stories tell of knights and cavalry officers of bygone days, especially in nineteenth-century Russia, and their principal theme is to extol codes of chivalry which have disappeared with the advent of mechanized armies and industrial society. It is the benign figure of the whimsical, slightly melancholy, and self-confessedly anachronistic Rittmeister who gives this work its unity. *Die Rittmeisterin* (1954) continues the theme and manner of *Der letzte Rittmeister*, and is a work ornamented with playful arabesques and allusions. The Rittmeisterin is the Muse who can fire a man with poetic dreams. The narrator meets in Geneva Musa Petrowna, who, born in Baltic Russia during the First World War, has been a displaced person virtually all her life. They exchange reminiscences of their mutual friend the late captain of horse. If Musa Petrowna cherishes the memory of the Rittmeister, Bergengruen can recall a summer of his boyhood by the Baltic coast which remains in his memory because of his devotion to the simple maidservant Anze.

Bergengruen has undoubtedly made a highly talented contribution to German fiction, impressive in its quantity and consistency. If he avoids the contemporary scene as a setting for most of his fiction, topical issues have sometimes appeared in his work in a disguised shape; above all, ethical problems of truth, justice, and love in their relationship to human frailty are his finest inspiration. Bergengruen's attitude to the novelist's craft is cool and professional; he has been able to illustrate the living quality of traditional approaches to narrative methods.

Born in 1876 of a Calvinist family that was on her father's side of French origin, Gertrud von le Fort began to publish her significant work after her conversion to Roman Catholicism; her verse *Hymnen an die Kirche* (*Hymns to the Church*), 1924, is of a devotional character. Through her father, who had been an officer in the German army before 1914, she was strongly impressed by the traditional conservatism of that period, and much of her writing shows her consciousness of its attractiveness while at the same time she rejects it as inadequate and misleading, in favour of an uncompromising commitment which, she believes, should suffuse all aspects of human life. Many of her stories have a historical setting, and in her use of the novelle she no doubt owes something to Conrad Ferdinand Meyer and Ricarda Huch. The tale *Die Letzte am Schafott* (English translation published as *The Song at the Scaffold*), 1931, shows the fear which overwhelms a young Carmelite nun when she is faced with martyrdom in Paris during the French Revolution. This work, translated into French by Bernanos, has formed the libretto of an opera by Poulenc. The heroine, whose extreme sensitiveness exposes her to onslaughts of despair and anxiety, has much in common with Rilke's Malte, and for Gertrud von le Fort's suffering women characters religious faith is the one bulwark against a nightmare world of neuroses, but at the same time it is no escape from personal responsibility. *Die Magdeburgische Hochzeit* ('The Magdeburg Wedding'), 1938, is a dramatically told novel of the resistance of Protestant Magdeburg during the Thirty Years War and its storming by Tilly's Imperialist forces. Violence in the name of religion appears to the author as an evil that is harder to accept as part of the ordering of the world than the conflicts of a later age, when the believer may be able to see himself as the victim of a form of worldliness that is to be rejected. *Das Schweißtuch der Veronika* (English translation of the first section published as *The Veil of Veronica*), 1928–46, is Gertrud von le Fort's principal work on a large scale. It is less obviously stylized than *Die Magdeburgische Hochzeit*, and follows the emergent development of a young woman. With detailed analysis and with clarity of exposition, the heroine's girlhood in pre-1914 Rome is presented, revolving round problems of faith; Veronika has been brought up in a secular environment by her grandmother, but is led to the Church by her own religious experiences. The second section of the novel takes place in Heidelberg soon after the end of the First World War. Here Veronika becomes engaged to Enzio, who has returned from the war disillusioned at his country's defeat. The incompatibility of Enzio's adherence to a Nietzschean outlook with Veronika's devout Catholicism forms the basic theme of the work. Veronika, highly strung and impressionable—she is known as 'Spiegelchen' because as a child she was a mirror open to all images and influences from outside—humble, weak and confined, earnest and innocent, embodies the female principle as the authoress conceives it, as complementary and yet opposed to the male. Enzio has been swayed by the teachings of Nietzsche and the Neo-Romantics, and his aesthetic concerns have become bound up with nationalist feelings. Liberal humanism is represented by the philosophy professor who is Veronika's guardian while she is in Heidelberg, though his approach has difficulties in face of the strongly held beliefs of the two young people. In spite of her guardian's advice, Veronika finally agrees to prepare for the marriage with Enzio. *Das Schweißtuch der Veronika*, by virtue of its closeness to the *Bildungsroman* tradition, unfolds in a broad, leisurely manner, but the sense of dramatic urgency is not lost.

Since 1945 Gertrud von le Fort has written fiction using more concentrated forms than the large-scale novel. The mood of these later works can be associated with her short essay 'Unser Weg durch die Nacht' ('Our Way Through the Night'), 1949, where the question of war-guilt is examined. Here she protests against the mass-conception of 'the Germans', insisting that every people remains a collection of individuals, and that Germans were capable both of crimes and of devoted humane helpfulness during the period when normal civilization broke down. Human weakness, she says, may not be glossed over, but neither may it be condemned out of hand. The four stories of the volume *Die Tochter Farinatas* ('The Daughter of Farinata'), 1950, centre on aspects of the struggle between worldliness and power on the one hand and resignation and love on the other. Bice, daughter of the dead hero Farinata, saves the city of Florence from destruction in the feuds between Guelph and Ghibelline—but by means of humility and outward defeat: 'And now that she had after all again be delivered to him wholly without protection, he became aware with deep emotion that there is nothing more inviolate than the unprotected, nothing holier than the unguarded. . . . For the will to destruction of this world shatters only against pity, and against nothing else.' Two tales *Gelöschte Kerzen* ('Extinguished Candles'), 1953, bring heart-searching conflicts of the time as a framework to two inset stories referring to the period of the Thirty Years War. 'Die Verfemte' ('The Outlawed Woman') recounts how a woman helped a Swedish officer to elude his captors and how her memory was regarded with shame by subsequent generations of her family; her deed, however, is vindicated in the situation of flight from the advancing Russians in 1945. 'Die Unschuldigen' ('The Innocents') centres upon the suffering of children during the last war, with particular reference to the village of Oradour. The narrator is a boy who ultimately goes mad and dies, as a result of too heavy a burden of fear and responsibility. The story *Am Tor des Himmels* ('At Heaven's Gate'), 1954, follows in its technique the manner of *Gelöschte Kerzen*; the arrest of Galileo by the Inquisition and his recantation of his astronomical discoveries are narrated from an old manuscript by a young man to a middle-aged woman as they shelter together in a cellar during an air-raid in Germany. Galileo's recantation is interpreted as an act of ironical defiance; if the Church refuses to face facts, he too will be cynical. His new interpretation of the cosmos is shown as having a significance for the seventeenth century which the discovery of nuclear fission has for our own time. The analogies with Brecht's drama *Leben des Galilei* are interesting to observe. Gertrud von le Fort is again concerned with persecution for conscience's sake in *Der Turm der Beständigkeit* ('The Tower of Constancy'), 1957. In eighteenth-century France, though intellectual life is worldly and sceptical, Huguenots are still incarcerated for their beliefs by a state that is nominally Roman Catholic. A sophisticated courtier is brought up with a shock by immediate experience of what this situation in fact may entail. *Die Frau des Pilatus* (*The Wife of Pilate*), 1955, illuminates the struggle between worldly and spiritual forces in the imagined relationship between Pontius Pilate and his wife when they are confronted by the challenge of the crucifixion. Again, it is the woman who follows the voice of the heart and finds salvation and martyrdom, while her husband is unable and unwilling to take this course. *Das fremde Kind* ('The Strange Child'), 1961, is more directly bound with German political and historical changes in the course of the twentieth century than most tales of Gertrud von le Fort. Two contrasting central figures, Caritas and Jeskow, form the chief support for the narrative structure. They come from a Prussian aristocratic milieu, which Jeskow accepts unquestioningly, while Caritas responds impulsively, without considering conventional attitudes, to her highly sensitive feelings of pity. The narrative has two main crises: the time of Jeskow's proposal to Caritas before the outbreak of the First World War, and the Second World War episodes of Jeskow's disillusionment and the death of Caritas. Gertrud von le Fort has here retained a traditional narrative style, while giving her own direct interpretations of important issues raised by events of the time.

Elisabeth Langgässer (1899–1950) showed already in her earlier published fiction that probing and complex style which was to become characteristic of her later work too. The first novel *Proserpina* (1932) describes forces of good and evil fighting for the soul of a five-year-old child; the work is a prose-poem using psychoanalytical and surrealist techniques. In short stories dating from the same year, for instance 'Mars', eruptive violence is uppermost. The novel *Der Gang durch das Ried* ('The Way Through the Marshland'), 1936, centres upon the son of a Mainz butcher who, terrified by his unbalanced father's sadistic tendencies, runs away and joins the French Foreign Legion, returning years later, in 1930, to the district of his childhood after being released from a mental home. He is still unbalanced, and tries in vain to fit his childhood memories into his adult personality as a French ex-soldier. In 1936 Elisabeth Langgässer was forbidden to publish by the Nazi authorities, and subsequently her daughter was deported to a concentration camp. It was not until 1946 that the authoress could bring out further published work, when her major novel, *Das unauslösliche Siegel* ('The Indelible Seal', English translation published as *The Quest*), made an immediate public impression. This work analyses the two crises in the life of a Jew who becomes a Roman Catholic—his denial of faith and consequent desertion of his wife and child in 1914, and his spiritual regeneration after his second wife has been murdered in 1925. The period between the two crises is a time when Belfontaine has denied his past and is attempting to live a life of cultured hedonism which shall deny all else but the present moment. It is not only a denial of his personal memory, but also of his national origin; the German who has been interned in France during the First World War marries into French provincial society and is wholly accepted there. Elisabeth Langgässer sees her hero as losing his way in barren wastes of triviality and despair, to be rescued by the miracle of grace. There are episodic elements, such as the retelling of the story of Bernadette of Lourdes, and the retelling of the problematic events in the life of Hortense, which do not appear to be immediately relevant to the main theme. *Märkische Argonautenfahrt* ('Argonauts' Journey in Mark Brandenburg'), 1950, a more compact novel, portrays a journey made in the summer of 1945 by a group of people from Berlin to a monastery in the Brandenburg country where some of them are to find the golden fleece of divine grace. Salvation is to be found through remembering, not forgetting, through awareness of individuality rather than through pantheistic merging into an impersonal whole. The concluding episode dealing with the corruption of a boy by a gang of black-marketeers recalls Graham Greene's underworld; there are points in common between Greene and Langgässer—their common faith as converts, their portrayal of the innocence and corruptibility of childhood, their preoccupations with sex and sin, with violence and crime— but these two novelists are poles apart in their narrative approaches, and Elisabeth Langgässer's complex prose-style and unusual vocabulary are much more ornate than Graham Greene's. She handles the interior monologue with a rhapsodical fervour which recalls Faulkner rather than Joyce. Faulkner's *A Fable*, that massive re-creation of Christ as the soldier whose resistance to trench warfare in 1914–18 leads to his martyrdom, might well be a novel which Elisabeth Langgässer would have liked to be able to call her own. The name of Bernanos also comes to mind when one considers Elisabeth Langgässer's sultry and confused vision of humanity caught up in the toils of irrational evil, though vouchsafed awareness of the divine.

Ina Seidel (born 1885) is a novelist for whom Protestant faith and nineteenth-century German traditions have been important factors in the building up of her imaginative world. *Das Labyrinth* ('The Labyrinth'), 1922, is a historical novel which reconstructs the life of Georg Forster, following him on his varied journeys and concluding with his death in Paris in 1794. Forster is interpreted as suffering in earlier life through his father's peculiar domination over him, and later through an unfortunate marriage. *Das Wunschkind* ('The Wish-Child'), 1930, is a family novel and historic panorama that has been very widely read in Germany. A mother-son relationship here receives idyllic emphasis, against the background of Germany during the period of the French Revolution and the Napoleonic wars. Cornelie von Echter loses her husband in the campaign against Revolutionary troops, while her son Christoph is to be killed in 1813. The relationship between French and Germans, between Protestant North Germans and Catholic South Germans is shown as problematic, but also as capable of positive resolution. *Unser Freund Peregrin*, (1940), less broad in scope than *Das Wunschkind*, conjures up an atmosphere of inwardness and sensitivity to the closeness of death and of a world of spirits. The narrator, Jürgen Brook, looks back to incidents from his youth, in particular to his meeting with the brother and sister Gregor and Tania, who introduce him to the poetic work and the supernatural presence of Peregrin, a fictitious author of the Romantic era who dies young. *Das unverwesliche Erbe* ('The Incorruptible Heritage'), 1954, is not wholly satisfying in its construction, but contains a thoughtful and considered portrayal of family relationships in a professional family towards the close of the last century. In her married life Elisabeth Alves suffers two serious depressive illnesses, both linked with her sense of guilt at having forsaken Catholicism and defied her father in order to marry Richard Alves. Her children are brought up as Protestants, but after the youngest, Maria, has been confirmed, Elisabeth wishes to return to the Church of her earlier years. No sudden resolution of the difficulties in her personality is possible, and time and other issues eventually give these problems a less urgent appearance. The arrival in the household of Elisabeth's mother, a serene otherworldly figure, has an enheartening influence upon all with whom she comes into contact. Maria's love for Joachim Lennacker and their brief married life introduce a young man of intellectual vigour into the family whose concern for a renewal of the Protestant Church is cut short by his early death. The final section, following Maria's widowhood and her devotion to her son, with the hesitancy and ultimate resignation in her relationship with the musician Jensen, seems less significant than the earlier sequences of the narrative. *Vor Tau und Tag* ('Before Dew and Dawn'), 1962, is a shorter work centring upon family life at the turn of the century, but starker and more concentrated in approach than *Das unverwesliche Erbe*. The principal character is Urd, shown in her growth from early childhood to late adolescence as threatened by the incursion of tragedy and yet able to develop without major hurt to herself. Her mother dies giving birth to her younger sister, and at a later stage her father, a medical practitioner, takes his own life. For Urd the figure of her father, who spends a long period in the tropics, is at times remote and bewildering, yet someone she wishes to admire and to approach more closely. *Michaela* (1959), broad and expansive in its manner, is the novel which more than any other shows Ina Seidel's reactions to the recent past. The principal narrator is the Jürgen Brook of *Unser Freund Peregrin*, now a widower in later middle age, who, deprived of his work as a librarian in 1933, lives for the most part as a private scholar. His chief personal contacts are with a group of like-minded contemporaries, in particular with Michaela, a widow living in Switzerland near the German border; with Muriel, who is prevented from continuing her private school in Germany after 1933 and takes up educational work in England; with Muriel's daughter Renée, whose husband Rainer spends the war years partly in concentration camp imprisonment and partly in the army; and with Einmann, a Berlin doctor, and his wife. In a discussion with Michaela, Jürgen Brook outlines his conviction that the German middle-class intelligentsia, as upholders of cultural values, formerly played a fundamental, non-militant role as an integrating and ennobling force in German society: '"Although this order manifests itself to all the world with words and works, with great deeds of the mind and spirit, only a few recognize that here there exists an order, a covenant, a great brotherhood."' This tradition of 'Brahmins' is linked by the narrator with the German Protestant heritage in particular, and he regrets that it has lost its vitality and effectiveness in recent times, and especially in face of the challenge of National Socialism. Michaela's estate, Merleberg, is linked by an underground tunnel to a farmstead within Germany. This suggests possibilities of outward action, and of the organizing of help for the persecuted, which are not realized in the course of the novel as fully as might be expected. A considerable part of the action takes place in Berlin, where Jürgen Brook and his friends share in the everyday life of people in the city, in particular during the war years. With the coming of peace in 1945 reconstruction can begin; Jürgen Brook has three active years as librarian, while the friends' educational concern can find fruition in a school to be established at Michaela's home.

Stefan Andres (1906–70) wrote as his first novel *Bruder Luzifer* (1932) which relates the experiences of a young artist who enters a Capucine order as a novice, but leaves after a year. One of the author's recurring themes is brought out here; the conflict between the moral order, as understood by Roman Catholicism, and the strong appeal of the senses. The tale centring upon an incident in the Spanish Civil War, *Wir sind Utopia* (*We Are Utopia*), 1943, is probably the author's best known work; it was forbidden publication in wartime Germany, but was clandestinely circulated at the time. The central character is a man who gives up life as a monk in order to work for his vision of an ideal world. An older priest appears to echo Andres's view when he tells him: 'Nobody has yet been able to reform the world and make a Utopia of it, nobody, not even God Himself! . . . He loves this world because it is imperfect.' The element of social and political criticism plays a considerable part in novels which Andres has written since 1945. *Die Hochzeit der Feinde* ('The Marriage of the Enemies'), 1947, treats the problem of Franco-German relationships. *Ritter der Gerechtigkeit* ('Knights of Justice'), 1948, is similarly motivated by a desire for a humane understanding that shall transcend national differences. It is set in Italy at the time of the fall of Mussolini; the author himself lived in Italy from 1937 to 1949. In the introductory chapter to *Das Tier aus der Tiefe* ('The Beast from the Depth'), 1949, the first volume of the trilogy *Die Sintflut* ('The Flood'), the narrator explains his intention of describing the Flood of our time, that is, the Nazi dictatorship. His method is to be one of realism, but in a Utopian setting, for he wishes to avoid the approach of complete fantasy on the one hand and topical reporting on the other: 'For the historical novel tries to awaken the dead, while journalism contents itself with the arrangement of what is already decaying.' Although it is a tale of corruption and greed for power, *Das Tier aus der Tiefe* is full of humour, and not the intellectual wit of G. B. Shaw, but the full-blooded humour of Dickens, as G. K. Chesterton distinguished them. The first volume shows the rise of the party from obscure origins under the leadership of Andres's archetypal dictator, the ex-priest Dr. Alois Moosthaler. The plot here is sustained by many ramifications, and if the sense of its inevitability is sometimes lacking, the author jumps clean over the gap with his exuberant fantasy. In the second part, *Die Arche* (1951), the dictator is in power as the 'Normer', threatening the freedom of individual development by his ruthless methods of standardization. A small circle of like-minded spirits attempts to sustain their independence of thought and action in face of the régime's increasing pressures; the concentration camp becomes a real part of these threats. A seriousness of mood has become dominant. *Der graue Regenbogen* ('The Grey Rainbow'), 1959, shows Central Europe shortly after the defeat of the dictator. There is a mood of confusion and depression, and hopes for the establishment of a new and better world, now that the Normer's state has disappeared, seem very slender. The parallels with the biblical story of the Flood are emphasized by the interspersing of legends concerning Noah in the narrative. *Die Reise nach Portiuncula* ('The Journey to Portiuncula'), 1954, links the author's familiarity with Italian backgrounds with the Germany of the new economic recovery. A prosperous middle-aged German brewer takes a holiday in Italy and returns to the place where thirty years before he betrayed a simple Italian girl and, with her, his youthful ideals of Franciscan poverty. Sulpiz Kasbach is a clever and rounded portrait, indicating the author's summing-up of a German business man of the early 1950s. The analogy between a biblical story and twentieth-century life which belongs to the framework of *Die Sintflut* is again developed in *Der Mann im Fisch* (1963). The main action centres upon the Hebrew prophet Jonah, while a secondary section shows the confrontation of Jonah with his modern counterpart Calame, whose life-story reveals comparable stresses and searching. After gaining fame as a prophet in his younger years, Jonah has disappeared, out of revulsion against the aftermath of his own attitude at that time. Twenty years later, he resents his identity becoming known again, and takes flight both from what the king expects of him and from what he hears Jehovah urging upon him from within his heart. The adventures of Jonah in Philistia and in the Mediterranean are recounted with verve. The interlude outside time, in the fish, leads to the paradoxical fulfilment of the prophet's mission when he preaches to the people of Nineveh. If Calame loses his faith when he hears of the dropping of the atomic bombs on Japan, and regards mankind as a 'week-end product of time and chance', the robust Jonah speaks of his life finally as 'the story of the self-righteous, misanthropic prophet of doom who brought grace to Nineveh against his own will and who was then converted by the repentant city to the recognition of the unlimited, omnipresent kingdom of grace'. The problems of the twentieth century challenge the prophet anew.

Edzard Schaper was born in Ostrowo in the province of Posen in 1908, settled in Estonia in 1930, fled from there to Finland in 1940 and moved to Switzerland in 1947. His early tale *Die Arche*, *die Schiffbruch erlitt* ('The Shipwrecked Ark'), 1935, is charming and whimsically sad in its description of the disastrous fate of a circus of wild animals that is being shipped from Sweden to Germany. In the novel *Die sterbende Kirche* ('The Dying Church'), 1935, Schaper describes the struggles of a faithful few to keep alive Orthodox Christian worship in a little Estonian town which in the years after 1918 became indifferent, if not hostile, to this community. The devotion and simple humility of Father Seraphim, an old priest, is touchingly portrayed. The dome of the church collapses during the solemn Easter service, causing the death of Father Seraphim and of some members of the congregation; disaster marks the end of this church community's separate existence, and symbolizes too the decline of the Orthodox faith as a whole. *Der letzte Advent* (1949) is a sequel to *Die sterbende Kirche*; it shows the efforts of Sabbas, who has been Father Seraphim's deacon and now feels weighed down with guilt at not having prevented the Easter calamity, to take an active part in extending his church's power. Quixotically he makes an illegal entry into Russia where he works secretly to spread the persecuted faith, only to be captured and to be faced with death. In his prose fiction Schaper frequently looks back to events in a Baltic environment either from the recent past of his own lifetime, or to earlier times when this area was under Tsarist rule. One of his recurring themes is the suffering of the political prisoner and the need for a schooling in stoicism which he sees as the lot of modern man. This message may be found in his two historical novels set in the France of the Napoleonic era (*Die Freiheit des Gefangenen*, 'The Freedom of the Captive', 1950; *Die Macht der Ohnmächtigen*, 'The Power of the Powerless', 1951). *Attentat auf den Mächtigen* ('Attempted Assassination of the Man of Power'), 1957, centres upon a visit of the Tsarist statesman Pobedonostsev as an old man to a German spa in 1901. The German police have instructions to provide him with personal protection, as he is known to be a target for revolutionary agitators. The planned assassination does not materialize; a young woman associated with the would-be assassin has a change of heart and remains for a time as confidante and companion to Pobedonostsev. The administrative arrangements of the police provide a quietly humorous framework to the central story. *Der vierte König* ('The Fourth King'), 1961, in an altogether more serious mood, relates an episode from the time of the German army's advance towards Leningrad during the Second World War. A group of the army come into close contact with a number of priests who have given shelter to homeless refugees. The abbot narrates a legend concerning a fourth Russian king who wished to join the three kings from the Orient visiting the infant Jesus. A Russian émigré Armjaninow, who is attached to the German forces, undergoes a transforming experience of religious dedication in consequence of his encounter with the monastic community. But when winter snow comes and the army has to yield to orders from the Nazi Party, the temporary idyll is dissolved; the activities of Russian partisans are responsible for the final disasters. This is a quietly moving novel, successful in its evocation of a particular mood, where the community of monks and refugees live precariously exposed to the threats from the contrasting atmosphere of war activity.

The main work of Hans Carossa (1878–1956) emanates from the decades well before 1945, and is often seen in the sequence of volumes of autobiography which opened in 1922 with *Eine Kindheit* (*A Childhood*), a quiet evocation of early years in a rural Bavarian setting, and was followed by *Verwandlungen einer Jugend* ('Transformations of a Youth', English translation published as *Boyhood and Youth*), 1928; experiences of a medical student are described in *Das Jahr der schönen Täuschungen* (*The Year of Sweet Illusions*), 1941, while the concluding volume, *Der Tag des jungen Arztes* ('The Young Doctor's Day), appeared in 1955. The proximity of this undertaking to Goethe's autobiography in approach is evident, as is Carossa's writing in other contexts also. This major work of Carossa's is episodic in form, and not fiction. An atmosphere of harmony and serene acceptance characterizes the novel *Der Arzt Gion* (*Doctor Gion*), 1931; the maid Emerenz who wishes to bear her child although this is

The Modern German Novel 1945-1965

likely to cause her death exemplifies such quiet resignation. *Geheimnisse des reifen Lebens* ('Secrets of Mature Life'), 1936, takes the form of first person narrative in which Angermann, a man in middle life living in retirement with his invalid wife Cordula, has an association with a woman who wishes to bear his child. The volume *Ungleiche Welten* ('Unequal Worlds'), 1951, is an account of its author's experiences during the Nazi régime. 'The German man of letters in the totalitarian state had become a suspect figure', he writes here. 'He was compelled either to be silent or at least to pass over in silence very essential phenomena of the contemporary world. Whichever attitude he assumed, from the non-German point of view he appeared either as provincially limited or as false.' Carossa notes with disapproval that soon after the end of the war voices could be heard hoping that a Third World War between Russia and America and Britain would come about, so that Germany might profit from it; or that the persecution of the Jews would soon be forgotten, or shrugged off as something admittedly terrible, but surely no worse than the cruelties of other nations and periods. Carossa's retrospection upon the Nazi period does not offer simple solutions to political problems, but like Gertrud von le Fort this author thought in terms of a 'great lifting of the hearts' without which 'no bread grows in the fields. Let each man be reconciled with himself; a time will come when he will be alone with his own soul.' As a pendant to *Ungleiche Welten* Carossa added a tale which gives an impression in narrative form of the summer of 1947. 'Ein Tag im Spätsommer 1947' conjures up the abnormally dry summer of that year in a Germany still in a condition of extreme exhaustion after the exceptionally hard winter preceding it. Set in the Bavarian countryside, there is unfolded to us the natural beauty of the landscape and the confusion in people's lives from the point of view of an elderly couple who maintain their serenity in spite of the unusual conditions of life all around them. Although there may be much evil and brutality in the world, it is implied, the opportunities for acts of loving kindness are multiplied and their value is always the same.

'. . . After all there may still be a hope'

An elegiac mood runs through the prose of Ernst Wiechert (1887–1950), with its delineation of dark moods and emotional inwardness, and its mourning for the disappearance of the idyll from contemporary life. An autobiographical account of his early years entitled *Wälder und Menschen* ('Forests and People'), 1936, recalls the East Prussian countryside of his childhood. Already a well known author in the 1930s, his expression of opposition to National Socialism led to his internment in a concentration camp for a period in 1938. In his short tale 'Der Hauptmann von Kapernaum' ('The Captain of Capernaum') he had condemned militarism and the old order of Germany in the name of a non-institutional Christianity. Life in the modern city is seen as degenerative in its effects on man's personality; withdrawal from this environment to the unspoilt, spontaneous simplicity of a remote countryside will have a healing effect as in *Das einfache Leben*, (*The Simple Life*), 1939. After 1945 Wiechert published two large-scale novels. *Die Jerominkinder* (English translation published as *The Earth is Our Heritage*) 1945-7, takes a village community in East Prussia as its background; the Jeromins are a family of fishermen, for generations in the service of the local landowner. Jons Ehrenreich Jeromin, gifted youngest son of this family, is enabled to go to the Gymnasium in the nearest town; after experiencing the First World War as a medical orderly, he continues studying, and then settles down in his native village as a general practitioner. The village stays happily apart from much of the unrest of the times, but it cannot avoid being subjected to the Nazi state; the novel ends in the year 1939, with the community on the brink of new terrors. The book is less a portrait of an age than a document of the emotions, above all, of its author's omnipresent anxiety about the problem of evil in the world of a good Creator; the basis of the questioning is the Book of Job, and the quotation prefixed to the novel is the line 'With God is terrible majesty'. *Missa sine Nomine* (1950) has as its principal theme the rehabilitation of three brothers whose lives have been disturbed by events leading up to the end of the war in 1945. They are from a land-owning family in East Prussia, and together with peasant farmers for whom the patriarchal relationship is still a living reality, they have become refugees from the East, living in a displaced person's camp. Ägidius's marriage to the widow of a farmer enables him to resume the kind of life to which he is best suited. Erasmus is less successful in his marriage and in his efforts to look after the welfare of the camp for displaced persons. For Amadeus, who has spent a period of four years in a concentration camp, the healing process is slower, but in time bitterness is replaced by serenity and love; his relationship with the seventeen-year-old Barbara, who clings long to her Nazi beliefs, indicates, not altogether convincingly, one facet of Amadeus's struggle for self-renewal. Wiechert recalls Thomas Hardy in a number of his themes and moods—his love of nature and sensitivity to its atmosphere, his sense of pity, his predominantly autumnal and elegiacal view of the universe. His picture of society has no place for urban technology nor for complex organization in administration; there should be a break-through of emotional directness and spontaneous idealism in human relationships. Wiechert's style is often elevated and lofty, for some tastes too much so, and the musical, lyrical element plays a considerable part in his writing.

The Novelle by Hanna Stephan (born 1902), *Der Dritte* ('The Third Man') recounts an episode during the flight of East Prussian country-people before the advance of the Russians in the winter of 1945. This tale is reminiscent of Wiechert's manner and motifs, just as Otto Heuschele's *Musik durchbricht die Nacht* ('Music Breaks Through the Night'), 1956, recalls the lyrical restlessness of Hesse's work and expresses a comparable dissatisfaction with the industrial age. Bernt von Heiseler (born 1907) reflects more closely an atmosphere of Lutheran Protestantism in his work. *Apollonia* (1940), a love story in a peasant setting during the First World War, recalls Gotthelf's tale of the French invasion of Switzerland in 1798, *Elsi, die seltsame Magd* ('Elsi, the Strange Maid'). *Versöhnung* ('Reconciliation'), 1953, is an extended chronicle showing the fortunes and misfortunes of a wide circle of friends during the Nazi period. Public events such as the assassination of Röhm in 1934, Neville Chamberlain's meetings with Hitler in 1938, the attempt on Hitler's life in 1944, and the defeat of Germany are neatly worked into a complex mesh of plot. A country estate in Bavaria forms the focal point in the lives of a family and their friends. Lutheran Christianity is in the forefront, though Heiseler has fewer misgivings than Wiechert in associating the church with the upper-middle class and a military tradition. The most convincing of the many plots and sub-plots which comprise the action is the account of a Lutheran pastor's struggles to maintain his integrity in face of political persecution.

Like Döblin, Kasimir Edschmid (1890–1966) first became known as a representative of the Expressionist generation. Soon after the war he brought out *Das gute Recht* ('One's Proper Right'), 1946, a novel which recounts the irritations besetting a family's life in war-time. An author and his family live during the war in a Bavarian village, where they have an uncongenial family billeted on them. Rotenhan, the author, unable to express himself during the Nazi régime, has devoted himself to writing travel-books; that he should have to share a house with Ziema, an unsympathetic supporter of this régime, is understandably a situation fraught with tensions. This record of the day-to-day difficulties of evacuation has value as a picture of the time. *Der Zauberfaden* ('The Magic Thread'), 1949, follows the story of the artificial-silk industry in Wuppertal and of the families associated with it. With *Wenn es Rosen sind, werden sie blühen* ('If They Are Roses, They Will Flower'), 1950, Edschmid wrote a fine historical novel which is concerned with the opposition struggles against the Hessian régime in the 1820s and 1830s. The reader's attention is directed less towards Georg Büchner, who takes flight to Strassburg at what transpires to be the expedient moment, but rather towards Ludwig Weidig, the idealist who stays to face arrest, torture, and death. In a study in novel form of the political and military career of Simon Bolivar (*Bolivar*, 1965; earlier edition, 1954) Edschmid discusses his hero's activities in three major sections. The account, consisting to a considerable extent of first-person narrative in diary form, plunges immediately into events of the civil war. The flight from Venezuela, the expedition up the Magdalena river, the re-entry of Venezuela from Colombian soil, and the triumphal progress to Caracas in 1813 form an effective unity. The Spanish general Morillo appears as the principal antagonist in Edschmid's second section, which concludes with the truce of 1820. The action widens to include the expeditions to Peru and Ecuador and the establishment of Bolivia. The hero's last years are shown as threatened by illness and by problems of internal government. Now the liberator is mistrusted by those who believe that too much power is centred upon one man; Bolivar asks: 'Have I really loved power without thinking that it is only the means of serving human dignity?' The reunion between the claims of freedom and order is not capable of easy solution, nor is the problem of the place of inhumane methods in the struggle for humane ends. *Whisky für Algerien* (1963) has as its narrator an art-dealer whose home is on the French-Swiss frontier of Geneva; his international affiliations, with air travel and long-distance telephone calls, seem to break down the more usual hazards to communication. In a contemporary milieu of prosperity and culture, where Expressionistic works of art have become exciting financial investments, a harsh intrusion from an alien sphere takes place. The protagonist's wife Cony loses her life in consequence of her involvement, out of motives of disinterested sympathy, with political conflict in Algeria. 'If I wish for freedom and a better world, I have to make my way through this sadistic age', one of the politically committed characters says. Edschmid's last novel is a further assertion of the importance for him of humane values.

Gottfried Benn (1886–1956) offered in his lyrical poetry, from the collection *Morgue* of 1912 onwards, verse where disillusioned pessimism most frequently dominates, expressed in a concentrated formal skill and lyrical richness, with an often esoteric allusiveness. His 'Berliner Novelle', *Der Ptolemäer* (1949), consists for the most part of the ruminations of a Berlin beauty-specialist (his parlour is significantly called 'Lotos') who looks at life in 1947 with sardonic scepticism. Berlin is a destroyed Carthage now, and the future can promise at most luxury and mundane emptiness; the coming century will only allow, apart from the masses, two types, the criminal and the monk. Life is now cheap; an occasional murder or death in the streets from hunger and cold arouses no interest. What are the achievements of the human mind? Benn's protagonist dismisses the whole scientific outlook from Kepler and Galileo onwards as nugatory, and sees religion as self-deception. He is willing to accept the epithets of nihilist and cynic, and against the German classical idea of development of personality, Benn advocates the claims of the artist: 'Do not perfect your personality, but your separate works. Blow the world as if it were glass, like a breath from a pipe . . . The artist is the only man who can get the better of things and who can make decisions about them. All the other types just go on messing the problems up . . . that is why I said: the glass-blower.' The unreal city behind an array of literary and philosophical allusions recalls T. S. Eliot's *The Waste Land* or W. H. Auden's *The Age of Anxiety*; Benn wrote a foreword to the German translation of this latter work. With his forceful and elastic style that can absorb jargon and yet remain poetic, Benn became a figure of considerable influence after 1945.

Max René Hesse (1885–1952) was concerned with the portrayal of pre-1914 society in the trilogy *Dietrich Kattenburg*. Independent of literary and political fashions, he lived for much of his life in South America. The development of his hero as a boy (*Dietrich und der Herr der Welt*, 'Dietrich and the Master of the World'), 1937, and as a young man (*Jugend ohne Stern*, 'Youth Without a Star', 1943; *Überreife Zeit*, 'Overripe Time', 1950) against the social background of his industrialist and officer family in the Lower Rhine area is probably autobiographical. With his high intelligence and his imaginative but unpredictably obstinate temperament, Dietrich has continuing difficulty in adjusting himself to the requirements of society as represented by his upper middle-class family and by the things they value. This is a solid, straightforward novel, distinguished by its rounded characterization and by its objective realism. The author stands away from his personages and their background, but portrays them with insight and acuity. The folly, intolerance, careless arrogance, hardness, and restlessness of these people are not condemned, but demonstrated in their actions; yet for all their faults, these characters lived in an age of security and of generally accepted loyalties, when the pattern of living was more rigid and thus possibly simpler for some than in later times. With its emphasis on the emergence of the hero's character—Dietrich is introduced as a small boy, and departs after he has completed his university course and become a cavalry officer—this work is a *Bildungs-roman*; the large cast of subsidiary figures also succeeds in coming to life, and the author has deployed his personages and themes with calculated skill.

Mars im Widder ('Mars in Aries'), 1947, by Alexander Lernet-Holenia (born 1897), describes the mobilization of troops in August 1939, the advance of motorized units through Slovakia, the uncertain waiting at the frontier, the invasion on 1 September, and the collapse of Polish resistance before the oncoming German forces. The novel closes sixteen days later, when the campaign is over and the Russians are in occupation of Eastern Poland. The narrative also includes a love story and the strange private experiences of its hero, an Austrian officer. *Der Graf von Saint-Germain* (1948) consists almost entirely of the first-person narrative of Phillip Branis, a wealthy Austrian industrialist who feels impelled to write down the main preoccupations of his life during the last days before his country is invaded by Hitler's orders in 1938. Twenty years earlier he had murdered des Esseintes, whom he suspected of being his wife's lover. After her death, a little time after their marriage, Branis lives without inward peace, remaining estranged from his wife's child, though responsible for his up-bringing. In this episodic novel, with its hints of the supernatural and of links with the eighteenth century, the unity is given in the main by the anguished moods of the central figure. *Der Graf Luna* (*Count Luna*), 1955, follows the career of a business-man in Vienna, Alexander Jessiersky, who has had a measure of responsibility in causing a certain Graf Luna to be sent to a concentration camp.

This incident preys on his mind, and in the years after the end of the war he becomes increasingly convinced that Graf Luna is persecuting him. The irrational violence of his retaliation, which costs several people their lives, leads to his flight to Rome. The catacombs, where he disappears and is not found again, provide the setting for the opening and conclusion of the novel, in which unusual elements in plot contribute a quality of gruesomeness.

Ernst Jünger (born 1895) has for a long time, since the publication of his experiences during the First World War, been concerned with the analysis of man in the context of his social problems. He has gone his way from the 1920s onward, hesitating to associate himself with organized political or religious movements, but concerned with the structure of society. *Afrikanische Spiele* (*African Diversions*), 1936, delineates a boy's determination to shape a new life for himself by breaking away from family life and attempting to join the French Foreign Legion. *Auf den Marmorklippen* (*On the Marble Cliffs*), 1939, written in a careful and rich prose style which dispenses with dialogue, describes the downfall of a happy, easy-going community and its traditions before the unscrupulous encroachments of the Chief Forester. The two brothers are forced out of their studious seclusion by these circumstances, after certainty concerning the Chief Forester's concentration camp has been established. They escape to Alta Plana, where as refugees they wish to work against the Chief Forester, and where they can mourn the passing of the old, independent way of life. The setting of this work is difficult to place, for it is one lacking the usual landmarks of modern life, and yet containing associations of magic and fantasy within the older traditions; the Mediterranean colour of the coastal area contrasts with the bleaker interior country where the Chief Forester has his headquarters. Ernst Jünger's novel about the future, *Heliopolis* (1949) is more confident in its hope for the triumph of man's finer aspirations than *Auf den Marmorklippen*. The 'times of fire' belong to the past and have been followed by a sturdy growth of new hope, even though terror cannot be banished, and cruelty and violence are an accustomed part of life in Heliopolis. Lucius de Geer, the central character, sees conflict as inevitable to human life: 'In long times of peace, annoyance, unrest and tedium vitae spread like a fever. There had to be, perhaps ever since the time of Cain and Abel, two great races, each with a wholly different conception of happiness. And both continued to exist in mankind, taking the leadership by turn. Often both of them dwelt in the same breast.' In an extended introduction Lucius is seen on board the ship that is bringing him to Heliopolis, a city divided by the struggle for power between the Prokonsul, to whose élite Lucius belongs, and the Landvogt, whose dictatorship has undeniable popular appeal. The discussions and visits in which Lucius is involved in Heliopolis form part of his development, supplementing the teachings of Nigromontanus, magician and interpreter of the world in terms of organic unity, and of Pater Foelix, hermit and wise theologian. Lucius also finds himself drawn to a permanent relationship with Budur Peri, who belongs to the minority of persecuted Parsees. The assassination of Messer Grande, one of the Landvogt's men, leads to reprisals at the expense of the Parsees, and Lucius's raid on the Landvogt's prison-fortress is a retaliation. Finally Lucius has to leave Heliopolis, going to serve the Regent, a remote, but powerful and inspiring figure. In this Utopian novel technological progress has been subordinated to the wish to conserve the past, and there is confidence that an aristocracy of the intelligent may succeed in preserving an effective bulwark against mass demagogy. The work has a certain static quality and discursive character which detract from its narrative vigour, but its thought is far-ranging and ingenious.

Besuch auf Godenholm ('Visit to Godenholm'), 1952, and *Gläserne Bienen* (*Glass Bees*), 1957, do not describe a world in conflict, but a post-war situation as seen by ex-soldiers who have as yet to find their place in the changed world. The two protagonists of *Besuch auf Godenholm* are to be saved from despair by a visit to a Norwegian island where a sage-magician will provide them with a hidden power which is to restore meaning to their lives. *Gläserne Bienen* is a neatly satirical work, with implications already foreshadowed in Jünger's sociological study *Der Arbeiter* ('The Worker'), 1932. The former cavalry officer Richard in his search for employment applies to the organization of Zapparoni, a grey eminence whose films for children and mechanical toys assure him widespread popularity and create an aura of harmlessness about scientific inventions which may at the same time be used for weapons of mass destruction. Such inventions are 'the cowardly triumph of calculating brains over courage and life'. Human perfection and technological virtuosity are irreconcilable, the hero reflects: 'An uncanny but also fascinating brilliance lights up perfect mechanisms. They arouse fear, but also a titanic pride which can be brought low not by insight, but only by catastrophe.' However, 'We are all burningly concerned with the thought that after all there may still be a hope'. Jünger may well be claimed as an outstanding practitioner of Utopian fiction in modern German literature.

Heimito von Doderer (1896–1966) invites comparison with his elder Austrian contemporaries Broch and Musil in the breadth of his vision and the largeness of scale in which he could conceive the novel. In an autobiographical sketch appended to the story *Das letzte Abenteuer* ('The Last Adventure'), 1953, he refers to himself as profoundly disillusioned, capable of surprise at nothing after living through the collapse of four régimes, the Austro-Hungarian monarchy, the Russian Tsardom, the first Austrian republic, the dictatorships of Dollfuß in Vienna, and of the Kolchaks in Siberia. One of his earlier publications *Das Geheimnis des Reichs* ('The Secret of the Empire'), 1930, tells in novel-form of the experiences of Austrian prisoners of war in Russia and Siberia, with particular reference to the period of civil war between the Soviets and the White Russians. The novel *Ein Mord, den jeder begeht* ('A Murder that Everyone Commits', English translation published as *Every Man a Murderer*), 1938, has a contemporary, but not precisely localized setting. Conrad Castiletz, having pieced together the earlier mystery of his wife's sister's death, discovers that he himself was unwittingly responsible for it. His own death, supervening by chance, deprives him of the opportunity to live out the new life open to him after self-discovery. *Ein Umweg* ('A Detour'), 1940, is a historical novel taking place in Austria shortly after the end of the Thirty Years War, written in an ornate, almost precious style that seems remote from the vigour of his manner in his later work. The theme of the old and the new life is presented with sombre tentativeness in the fortunes of Paul Brandtner and of Manuel Cuendias, the latter being a Spanish aristocrat and intellectual. *Das letzte Abenteuer*, completed in 1936 but not published until 1953, is a Novelle with traditionally Romantic requisites in its fourteenth-century setting; here too the central character, Ruy de Fanez, undergoes a transforming experience and meets death very shortly afterwards. *Die erleuchteten Fenster* ('The Illuminated Windows'), 1951, is similarly a work written during the 1930s, a slight comedy in an urban milieu.

In such earlier works there is the feeling not only that their characters are struggling to discover the nature of the reality that they should confront, but also that the author himself has not yet completely discovered the appropriate vehicle for his imaginative thought. This he achieves triumphantly in *Die Strudlhofstiege* ('The Strudlhof Steps'), 1951, and even more generously and variedly in its sequel *Die Dämonen* (*The Demons*), 1956. A number of the characters appear in both novels, and the principal link is René von Stangeler, whose more restless earlier phase in *Die Strudlhofstiege* forms the complex prelude to the relative stability of the research historian in *Die Dämonen*. *Die Strudlhofstiege* alternates between two sets of incidents, the one period being 1910–13, the other being the summer of 1925. There is a welter of plot, characters, love-affairs, and business propositions, the work rising to a climax in the events of 21 September 1925. Mary K. is saved from death as a result of a tram accident by the prompt intervention of Melzer. His successful action here finally disperses the misgivings that have been haunting him for years, and he is able to begin a re-integrated life. He can now propose to Thea Rokitzer, and their marriage will initiate a 'new life'. Already before the ambulance has arrived, Melzer realizes that for Mary K. a life of a different kind will begin: 'This that was here was not death: Melzer knew death. What encircled this gentle head was rather the whole hardness of a life that was to come.' In the course of *Die Dämonen* Mary K. gradually overcomes her disability. Catastrophe has inevitably thrown her from the 'narrow-gauge tracks' of her earlier life, though the later coming together of Mary and Leonhard Kakabsa represents a new life for both of them.

Die Strudlhofstiege is concerned with memory and the private life, though the business intrigue of the immediate post-inflation years anticipates the wider scope of its sequel. Novels which are concerned with the rehabilitation of lost memories may well be slow-moving and replace dramatic incident by analysis and a broad delineation of associations of ideas. Doderer takes his time here too, but is self-disciplined in his combination of a loving lingering on half-forgotten impressions with a skilful deployment of many characters and plots. Inventiveness of plot-devices accompanies him all the time. In one respect *Die Dämonen* is simpler than *Die Strudlhofstiege*; its action takes over where the earlier work left off, and moves steadily forward to its climax of the general strike and the burning of the Palace of Justice on 15 July 1927, the principal action taking place in the nine months preceding this incident. The main narrator is Geyrenhoff, who has just retired in middle age from the civil service and who begins writing up the story in the spring of 1927 and has it finally ready in 1955. Doderer himself worked on the first section of *Die Dämonen* in the 1930s. The narrative is at times transferred to other hands than those of Geyrenhoff; Schlaggenberg, a professional novelist, makes his contribution. There are interpolations such as the 'night-diary' of Frau Kapsreiter, the 'chronique scandaleuse' of Schlaggenberg's investigation of fat ladies and a manuscript concerning the irregular detainment of two respectable middle-aged women on a trumped-up charge of witchcraft in the late fourteenth century.

The novel's title clearly harks back to Dostoievsky and to the Gospel story of the Gadarene swine. The demonic element in man and society is a constant threat to decency and civilization; the disreputable urges of a sick mind (and Doderer implies that to be subject in some degree to such sickness is part of the human condition) undermine the mental health of the individual, while on the level of the community as a whole political unrest and financial unscrupulousness have a comparable effect. But Doderer's optimism and sense of comedy win through, in spite of darker episodes and directions. If the one interpolated episode describes a man's temporary temptation to abuse the machinery of witchcraft trials, this might well have become a gruesome narrative, but instead it transpires to be comedy, though of a grotesque nature. Similarly the social unrest of July 1927, although seen from the public point of view as the 'Cannae of Austrian freedom', still conveys some sense of comedy. For the strike and the fire intervene in the lives of many of the characters with the effect of bringing about a profusion of happy marriages. While no solution to Austria's social and political problems is indicated, on the individual level there can be development, movement away from what the author calls a second reality, the world of illusion and fanaticism, to a first reality of common sense, stability and serenity. *Die Strudlhofstiege* and *Die Dämonen* are impressive for various reasons, but primarily as a picture of a world which is enormous in its range, extending to many varied aspects of society, and yet built up step by step with elaborate, detailed care as to style, plot, characterization, and background. We have here an outstanding and distinguished modern German novel.

Doderer published contributions to the theory of the novel, after the appearance of *Die Dämonen*, in the essay 'Grundlagen und Funktion des Romans' ('Foundations and Function of the Novel'), 1959, and among the diary entries of *Tangenten* ('Tangents'), 1954. The novelist's ultimate authority, he has said, is the world as it is. The novel as a genre is unique in its ability to present empirical reality. Knowledge of the world and of himself is required of the novelist, who must fuse these two forms of knowledge into something larger. The fruitful combination of inner and outer experience is only possible if man does not insist on forcing experience into preconceived moulds. However, Doderer sets himself apart from Joyce, Proust, and Musil, who, he infers, did not distinguish between the more and the less worthwhile material of life for their work; he puts himself at a distance from them too in his opposition to the dissolution of narrative into stream of consciousness or over-expansive analysis. But he associates himself with them in his contribution to a vision of the 'total novel'; in an age of increasing specialization the novel as a genre has a potential universality which no other genre can offer. Its author may use a totality of narrative techniques, as well as of material. Means to the ends of realism and totality are invention, action and memory. Doderer strongly disagrees with those who would contend that action in the novel is out of date, that analysis and intellectual thought are of prior significance. Memory is the chief factor of the creative imagination, and an author needs to be in a state of close imaginative accessibility to the material brought forward through recall.

After *Die Dämonen* Doderer's inventive powers, combined with a capacity to plan intricate large-scale narrative, continued undiminished. These qualities reveal themselves in the extremely concentrated and fantastic plot of *Die Merowinger, oder die totale Familie* ('The Merovingians, or the Total Family'), 1962. Baron Childerich von Bartenbruch, or Childerich III, hopes to bring about the total focusing of his family relationships upon himself; through a series of 'dynastic' marriages he comes almost within fulfilment of his aim, but is frustrated through the opposition of his major-domo Peppin and members of his family. In this novel farce and parody play a major part, and the action proceeds with hectically concentrated rapidity.

Die Wasserfälle von Slunj (1963) is the first section of what was intended to be Doderer's 'novel no. 7'. A new panorama of people and places unfolds here, with a time sequence of more than thirty-two years, beginning in 1877. There is a not unexpected combination of the grotesque and the serious. The dominating figures are two Englishmen, Ronald Clayton, who sets up a branch-factory for agricultural machinery in Vienna, and his son Donald who grows up into the Viennese background while remaining apart from it (boarding school education in England is followed by engineering training in Vienna). Donald is haunted by a sense of failure and depression when Monica Blacher, with whom he has earlier been reluctant to become emotionally involved, becomes his father's mistress, and when his subsequent approaches to another woman, Margot Putnik, are unsuccessful. While on holiday, shortly afterwards, he meets his death when he slips from the wooden bridge over the waterfalls. Donald Clayton's sense of unease at being torn between English and Austrian ways of life (where his father's relationship with Monica Blacher precipitates a sense of isolation and despair) recalls the situation of Manuel (in *Ein Umweg*), the Spaniard who is not wholly at home in seventeenth-century Austria. Although the process of transformation is withheld from Donald Clayton, it is a theme present in much of Doderer's fiction; undoubtedly this concept of 'Menschwerdung' ('development', 'humanization') has been a fruitful and central aspect of his writing. The relationship between illusion and reality is uneasy. The integration of imagination and practical realism ('Profundity is outside. The inner life is only a way towards it.'), though seldom attained, is essential and desirable for happiness and fulfilment.

Doderer published an admiring study of the artist and author Albert Paris Gütersloh, *Der Fall Gütersloh* in 1930. Gütersloh (born 1887), whom Doderer claimed to regard as his master, has made his own contribution to the Austrian 'total' novel with *Sonne und Mond* ('Sun and Moon'), 1962, a work whose genesis ran parallel to that of Doderer's *Die Dämonen*; Gütersloh had been working on this novel since 1935. Subtitled 'a historical novel from the present-day', it is a challenge in its intricate and highly involved style, in the frequently bewildering presentation of its incidents and in the fanciful accumulation of detail. Count Lunarin, the 'moon', and the prosperous farmer Till Adelseher, the 'sun', are complementary figures, both closely involved in the disposal of a castle and estate in Austria. Lunarin learns by chance of his inheritance, and returns from wanderings in Africa to see if the estate can be made of some use in restoring his finances. He appoints six domestic servants, asks Till Adelseher to be his manager, and then disappears. On his return about a year later (the time is the early 1930s) he finds that the dilapidated property has been renovated on the initiative and at the expense of Till Adelseher. Till is presented with it as a gift, which he accepts—a gesture which causes Melitta von Rudigier, living nearby, to transfer her affections from the former to the Count. The latter's elusiveness and exotic charm are in contrast to the farmer's more staid and stolid personality. Perhaps, interlocking together, they represent one facet of Austrian society. It is the inclusion of various retrospective episodes, however, which is likely to bewilder and at the same time to attract the reader. The author's heart seems to be not so much in the 1930s as in the pre-1914 era. The incidents may group themselves around the antecedents of the main characters, or around the locality of the district where the castle is situated. Owing to the experiences of a young woman, Benedikta Spellinger, in 1887, a monastery becomes for a while a place of pilgrimage. A painter, Andree, after quarrelling with his mistress, the wife of a rich Jewish banker, spends a memorable interlude in the country before finally leaving Austria for Paris. In 1902 Mullmann leaves his work as a customs officer and becomes attached to the Lunarin household; the city with its 'baroque character', 'its barbarian mother' and 'Roman father', is extolled in this episode. The waiter Murmelsteeg has an English wife and children who come from Folkestone to look for him in Austria. The relationship of Obdeturkis, another painter, with Melitta is in some respects a reflection, decades later, of Andree's connection with the banker's wife. Andree and Lunarin learn decisive news about their fortunes from old newspapers. Lunarin and Till Adelseher are both affected, in different ways, by their attitude to their mothers. The many-sided episodes and characters of *Sonne und Mond* all remain consistently within the sphere of comedy.

4 '. . . The basic assumption is no longer the same.' (Hans Erich Nossack)

SINCE 1945 a considerable number of novelists have become known for the first time in Germany. They include people who have been contemporaries of those whose published work was already available before 1939, but who did not themselves come forward as imaginative writers until the way seemed clear for a new start, or who, if they had published earlier, had not thereby become at all widely known and had not established a firm pattern for their further development as authors. Then there is the younger generation of those for whom the impulse and opportunity to write came after 1945. These are authors who have begun either afresh or for the first time to express themselves and to react to the world around them, without the assisting or the limiting factors of an earlier established public image to be borne in mind.

Hans Erich Nossack's (born 1901) *Nekyia. Bericht eines Überlebenden* ('Nekyia. Account of a Survivor'), 1947, plunges us into a dream-world which is to symbolize the transition between death and reincarnation, and in addition the interim period of chaos immediately after the collapse of Germany in 1945. As sole survivor of a dead city, the protagonist questions the relevance of time and memory: 'For what is actually said by the phrase "There lies something behind me"? Formerly there was nothing more reliable than chronology. Everything was exactly divided and could be expressed in figures. One man was thirty years old and another had been alive a thousand years ago. The calculation was right too, but the basic assumption is no longer the same. Time has been smashed. . . .' The narrator is a modern Orestes, and behind a soldier's return from war in or after 1945 stands the archetypal Agamemnon's homecoming from Troy. This 'Bericht' is so violently opposed to what E. M. Forster, in *Aspects of the Novel*, has called the 'chopped-off length of the tapeworm of time', that it ceases to be a story; the causal thread has gone. The volume *Dorothea* (1948) consists of 'Berichte', as if the author were wishing his work to be thought of as reporting, not fiction. A being from another planet who has been sent to observe the situation in Germany writes: 'The day lies behind them [humanity], and knowledge that was light to no purpose, makes them sceptical of everything. But how can one expect of beings who have no faith in themselves that they will come through the dark?' The bombing of Hamburg in July 1943 forms the central experience of the book, and is reported in 'Der Untergang'. It was then that Nossack lost most of what he had written up to that time, but had not published (he was forbidden to publish by the Nazi authorities). 'Interview mit dem Tode' relates sardonically conditions in Hamburg in May 1947; death is no longer a reaper, a veiled figure in black, or a consumptive young man—he is the blackmarketeer who is out and about at night, lies in in the morning, has his room heated in late spring and drinks real coffee.

Spätestens im November ('At Latest in November'), 1955, is a more sustained piece of narrative writing than any of the earlier pieces. The outline of this novel's action is simple; the wife of a wealthy industrialist falls in love with a writer whose work is just beginning to find recognition. She leaves her husband and child, lives for a time with the impoverished writer, returns after a few months to her family, but again goes off with her lover to meet death with him when he crashes in his newly acquired second-hand car. The author's social criticism is here directed against the captain of industry who is concerned with the amassing of wealth and power and with the wish to be regarded as a model business-man. The contrast between him and the man of letters is pointed. In its narrative method it is less experimental than the earlier works; the events are seen consistently from the woman's point of view, and unfolded with a bare directness of exposition. The division of loyalty between the business world and that of the artist is also the theme of *Der jüngere Bruder* (1958). An engineer who has returned to Germany after a ten-year absence in South America looks at the social scene in post-war Europe with critical misgivings. His search for his 'younger brother' extends to both East and West Germany, and is essentially a quest for the resolution of inward, personal problems.

Spirale (1956), subtitled 'novel of a sleepless night', is introduced as an account of man's holding judgement upon himself; the 'spiral of his thoughts' prevents his sleep by projecting fragments of his past life into his consciousness. The five narratives that follow can be linked with one another as episodes relating periods of inward crisis in one man's life. At the age of eighteen he looks back to the unhappy relationship between his parents ('Am Ufer', 'By the Riverside'). Three years later he decides to break away from student life in order to become a factory-worker ('Die Schalttafel', 'The Switchboard'). The most extended of these narratives, 'Unmögliche Beweisaufnahme' ('Inadmissible Evidence'), is a trial scene; the court wishes to establish an accused man's responsibility for the disappearance of his wife, for what he refers to as her 'setting out into the realm of the un-insurable', a state of being separated from the common-sense world. 'Die Begnadigung' ('The Pardon') shows the narrator in prison, where he is reluctant to accept the pardon that is offered to him, since he is terrified at the thought of leaving prison. 'Das Mal' ('The Mark') describes an expedition into a bare snow-covered landscape, and the decision not to proceed further into the unknown but to return to life and normality. It seems as if this final spiral has moved from the setting of a man who feels hemmed in by the environment of humdrum urban living into its visionary alternative, a cold challenge that impels the explorer to return to the familiar. In the story 'Der Neugierige' ('The Inquisitive One', in the collection of stories *Begegnung im Vorraum*, 'The Meeting in the Hallway', 1963) Nossack portrays the situation of the questioning solitary individual and his need to break through to a fuller reality than that which satisfies his contemporaries; here the fable of a fish venturing from the sea on to dry land strikingly illustrates the author's theme.

Nach dem letzten Aufstand ('After the Last Uprising'), 1961, has several narrative clusters and a complex framework-technique. Alois Mörtl, the principal narrator, has changed his role in life more than once; after years as a waiter, abroad and then at home, he was chosen to be 'companion to the god', and subsequently, having survived 'the last revolt', has been nightporter at a Munich hotel. Part of the bewildering but compelling atmosphere of this novel may lie in the combination of an unsurprising, present-day realism of background with a sequence of fictitious public events. Alois Mörtl writes his account during a period of settled, secular sobriety which can congratulate itself on having overthrown an earlier society that placed great emphasis on a religious cult that now appears cruel, meaningless, and superstitious. The last young 'god', however, behaves as if divinely inspired and bewilders the 'supreme servant', who is accustomed to exploiting the institution for his own ends. The shorter work *Das kennt man* ('That Is Known'), 1964, centres upon a Hamburg prostitute; apart from her partisan unstable role on the fringe of society, she has been involved in another alien way of life that threatens her. An inward refusal to absorb the outlook of the majority, especially if this involves conformity to the state and to mass-society, has been seen by Nossack as an attitude to which the intellectual should be committed.

Die Stadt hinter dem Strom (*The City beyond the River*), 1947, by Hermann Kasack (1896–1966), is a vision not of an imagined future, but of a life beyond death; its atmosphere reflects aspects of the Germany of the period during which the novel was written. The carefully constructed world of this fantasy bewilders the stranger who finds himself plunged into it. Robert Lindhoff finds himself alien to the pattern of life in this perplexing city, where most activities are carried on underground, while the streets above are mostly deserted and the houses in ruins. He cannot understand the reasons that compel subservience to a mysterious higher authority. The theme of the stranger in an alien, puzzling world is one that recalls Kafka's novels. It is not until half way through the book, after the love scene with Anna, that Lindhoff discovers that he is the only living person in a city of the dead, and that the others have but a short time to wait before their spirits are dissolved in the All. Like Hermann Hesse, Kasack felt drawn to Eastern mysticism; he expounds his vision of the relationship of life and death in pantheistic terms. The novel indicates that Western civilization is heading for disaster, and that the world can only be saved by a reestablishment of the spiritual and intellectual supremacy of the East, which shall counter 'the deadly poison of reason' and the misuse of technological inventions. The earlier half of the work, where Lindhoff is introduced to conditions in the city, keeps up the suspense well, and the description is rounded and plastic. The later sections, where political and social comment plays a large part and where the author's underlying thought is expounded in more detail, are more abstract. *Das große Netz* ('The Big Net'), 1952, is a satirical novel concerned with the demoralizing effects of a materialistic hedonism in the Hollywood style. A community, having been sealed off from the larger world, is taken over by an organization IFE, a name which stands not for the Nigerian university town of Ife, nor for 'Institute for Europe', but for 'International Film Export'. The loosely strung together episodes are seen largely from the point of view of Icks, a sales representative who drifts into close co-operation with this enterprise. As a novel this work is altogether less impressive than *Die Stadt hinter dem Strom*. Kasack's *Fälschungen* ('Forgeries'), 1953, set in the German background of its time, centres upon an episode in the life of a middle-aged business-man who has long devoted energy and enthusiasm to collecting old wood-carvings. The discovery that his collection includes forged work and that in consequence unjustified suspicions are directed upon his good will brings about a crisis in his personal life that is sensitively described.

Heinz Risse (born 1898) is on the whole traditional in his approach to style and narrative methods. He is less concerned with poetic prose than with the depiction of action in quick-moving, bare lines. Melodrama, and occasionally fantasy, go side by side with everyday realism. His first publication, *Irrfahrer* ('Man

Adrift'), 1948, is described as a Novelle; this story of a prisoner-of-war and his re-orientation in the peace-time world does not as yet reveal the qualities which make Risse's first novel, *Wenn die Erde bebt (The Earthquake)*, 1950, and its successor, *So frei von Schuld* ('So Free of Guilt'), 1951, distinctive. These works are 'philosophical tales' in the sense of Voltaire's *Candide* or *Zadig*, and seem to have a further hinterland in preoccupations with Calvinist predestination; the melancholy artistry of Gottfried Benn has fascinated the author. *Wenn die Erde bebt* has as its central character a man who can foretell the future; it is ironical that someone with such gifts should be employed in an insurance office, where, however, he annoys the management by his refusal to put his services at the firm's disposal. He dislikes what he calls the elephantiasis of capitalism just as much as communism, which he considers its equally materialistic opposite. When the earthquakes come and the fabric of civilization is torn, he is glad, for disaster brings a new spirit of friendship and helpfulness among people. But when order is restored, the old pushing, uncharitable selfishness reasserts itself, and the protagonist is once more the eccentric outsider. *So frei von Schuld* is about a man whom a variety of unmerited disasters befall—a twelve years' sentence for a crime he has not committed, the loss of his only child in a railway accident, his wife's death through illness, the more general confusion through invasion (the country is split in two after being overrun by a military organization that is pledged to the abolition of wealth and religion). Risse's first novel, showing the earthquakes in their physically and psychologically disintegrating effect on conventional society, reflects the impact of the war on German life, though it may be queried how close the analogy can be between a series of natural calamities and the man-made disasters of war. *So frei von Schuld* has as its social background the division of Germany into two by occupation forces. *Dann kam der Tag* (1953), is a criticism of the managerial mentality and the plutocratic conception of success. In *Wenn die Erde bebt* the protagonist has murdered his wife, and is under medical observation; *Dann kam der Tag* has as its central figure a man of seventy, who has attempted to set fire to the factory which he owns. After a life-time of fighting for money and power the old man realizes that he has lost emotional sincerity and moral principles, and regrets this loss; his belated efforts to turn in a new direction are regarded by those around him as manifestations of senility.

Große Fahrt und falsches Spiel ('Long Journey and False Play'), 1956, is set in the nineteenth century. The initial impulse to the action is a bizarre situation; a small group of sailors, shipwrecked on an inhospitable island, feel driven to planning the killing of one of their group in desperate hunger. From this enclosed narrative situation the author leads the reader, through a series of unexpected happenings, to a conclusion which further emphasizes the themes of retribution, justice, and revenge and the enigma of determinism and free will. It is a sombre picture of human nature, revealed all the more harshly in a setting where the forces of nature seem particularly threatening. *Ringelreihen* ('Round Dance'), 1963, centres upon its hero's fervent wish to be disengaged from all ties to society. He writes his story while in prison, knowing that he will soon be shot. Having been compelled to act as an interpreter at interrogations when a civil war breaks out, he is later made a prisoner himself. Neither side in the war wins his confidence in their aims, and one form of police state is no more attractive than another. The later and larger section of the novel consists of interrogation scenes, where the subject of the relationship of the individual to society is debated. Although *Ringelreihen* is rather loose in construction and lacks definition in its background, it is a serious and thoughtful novel. Risse's inventive plots repeatedly direct our attention to concepts of order and chaos, justice and punishment, conscience and guilt, providence and chance.

Werner Warsinsky's *Kimmerische Fahrt* ('Cimmerian Journey'), 1953, presents an analysis of a mind that has become deranged by war which recalls Langgässer's *Der Gang durch das Ried*, and a poetically stylized vision of the transition from life to death which has something of the manner of Broch's *Der Tod des Vergil*. Warsinsky succeeds in informing the stream of consciousness structure with colourful language and with a realistic background of the war in Russia and of the broken man's groping for life in post-war Germany, helpless as he is in his search for a reintegrated personality. His journey to the land of constant darkness allows of no safe return to the world of light and normality. This work, although not altogether free from obscurities in its effects, contains many isolated passages of power.

In a letter from Berlin dated 28 March 1945, Friedo Lampe (1899–1945) wrote:

What times these are! I try more and more to regard this age and its terrible happenings as a process of purification. We should say goodbye to everything, be bound no longer to what is earthly, and should look at life as if we had already died. We should learn to conquer fear of life as of death. The hope of a sensible and happier life is surely very slight. The whole of Germany is after all a heap of rubble. Continuity with the past has been destroyed. None of this can be made good again. No, we may not think further along these lines. We must learn to think on other lines, but that is very painful and difficult, especially for people like myself who live through sense impressions. Right at the end may be seen beckoning a freedom and happiness, a feeling of being separated from all that is material, and an insight into the infirmity and transience of earthly things which earlier generations have experienced only in rare comparable moments.

The author of these lines, which were penned no doubt in distracted haste and anguish, reflects in his few but delightfully written stories a spirit of sensitive fantasy and humour that recalls the manner of Robert Walser. His work has only become known at all widely in the volume of his Collected Works (1955), since his death. For he was shot by Russian troops on 2 May 1945, through a misunderstanding in the first days after the occupation of Berlin. His sparkling, iridescent prose reflects atmosphere, colour, and the sensation of things, as in the short story 'Am Leuchtturm' ('At the Lighthouse'), with its impressions of a summer day at a North Sea seaside resort.

Ernst Kreuder (born 1903) is concerned with the vindication of fantasy, which with its rejection of the everyday world can look towards the establishment of a happier community. *Die Gesell-schaft vom Dachboden* (English translation published as *The Attic Pretenders*), 1946, has a literary programme; it is critical of natural-ism and the proletarian novel on the one hand, and on the other of the intervention of philosophy and abstraction (summed up in the word 'Tiefsinn', 'profoundness') in literature. Laurel and Hardy, Charlie Chaplin, and Westerns appeal to the members of this secret society as more stimulating models; one is reminded here of the juxtaposition of James Joyce and Zane Grey in Graham Greene's *The Third Man*. The society meets in an attic lumber-room with the purpose of combating the limitations of everyday realism and middle-class conventionality by means of the imagina-tion. The immediate post-war situation is the background here. *Die Unauffindbaren* ('Those Who Cannot Be Found'), 1948, expands the programme of *Die Gesellschaft vom Dachboden*, which it indicates through an opening quotation from Jean Paul: 'Literature is not a flat mirror of the present, but the magic mirror of a time which does not exist.' An estate-agent leaves his wife and two children one Sunday afternoon just before tea and drifts into series of adventures involving him in a society of people who defy the claims of the common-sense world. The background of the action is American, but this is only lightly sketched in, perhaps to prevent the reader from seeking props in the everyday world. The whole action may be the ramblings of a mind which in the delirium of an illness escapes from the ties of reason and responsibility into the liberating fluidity of fantasy, the true fulfilment of the unconscious mind. The gossamer tenuousness and effortless limpidity of Kreuder's prose, its containment of colloquialisms within an enveloping lyricism are qualities that may be found also in the style of Henry Green or L. P. Hartley. *Herein ohne anzuklopfen* ('Come In Without Knocking'), 1954, is more explicit than *Die Unauffindbaren* in its approach; the author's criticism of modern European life includes a plea for the quiet, contemplative way of the Eastern mystics. The narrator makes his way from a moving train to a mental home, where there is a community of those who learn to liberate themselves from the

hectic routine of modern industrial society. The 'big three'—
birth, fate, and death—will in any case insist on coming in without
knocking. There is a nice spirit of fun and irony to leaven the
didactic element. We must recapture our lost innocence:

'Something must have got lost at some time, something in us, a
sense which once affected us so that things were not as they are now,
and that we were all right.'
'Can't we find this sense again?'
'It has not only got lost,' I said, 'I am afraid it has been destroyed and
has left us.'
'Who destroyed it?'
'Our thinking,' I said, 'that is, we ourselves. With our thinking we
have driven out and destroyed something that is older than ourselves,
that is as old as eternity.'
'How do we know about it then?'
'There are still traces of it to be found in the myths and fairy-tales.'
'What is it then?' she asked.
'Innocence,' I said. . . .

Agimos oder Die Weltgehilfen ('Agimos or the World Helpers'),
1959, centres upon a group of people who have come to dissociate themselves from much that is characteristic of modern
life; there is a rejection of 'so-called exact thinking' because it
destroys delicacy of feeling and positive appreciation of nature
and the world of the senses. Mass-society must overcome its
drive to mass-destruction, and the surface illusion of urban smart-
ness must not be allowed to obscure the inevitable presence of
death. The author weaves together a series of episodes, illustrating
various problematic situations into which individual characters
have been thrown, with the presentation of social diagnosis and
ideas in conversation or lecture form. These elements are placed
within the larger framework of an escape-story in a Balkan
country. Two German visitors are captured by insurgents, but
succeed in getting away to a major city; here contact is made
with a secret organization, and the later section of the narrative
concentrates upon Asbjörn Friderik's relationship with Berenice,
the crossing of the frontier and the return to his home near

Heidelberg. Friderik has given up his regular practice as a psychiatrist and acquired an old country house which he uses as a home for the rejected. Ernst Kreuder presents the whole with a lyrical sensibility of style that is particularly his own.

Like Mörike, of whom he has written a short study, Albrecht Goes (born 1908) is a native of Württemberg and a Protestant pastor. Two Novelle of his made an immediate impression by their direct sincerity and economy of presentation. *Unruhige Nacht* (English translation published as *Arrow to the Heart*), 1949, narrates an episode from the campaign in Russia as seen by an army chaplain. *Das Brandopfer* (*The Burnt Offering*), 1954, shows how a butcher's wife, while serving the weekly meat ration during the war, comes to realize fully the cruelty of the plight of Jews in Nazi Germany. The tale is a memorial, erected in a spirit of forgiveness, not of bitterness: 'To conjure up what has happened in the past; but for what purpose? Not in order to prolong hatred.' Goes's writing and care for form are precise, and his expression of an ideal of forgiveness and tolerance is framed in terms which have made these two tales compelling both to English and German readers.

Kurt Ihlenfeld's (born 1901) *Wintergewitter* ('Winter Thunder'), 1951, evokes the atmosphere in a Silesian village in February 1945. The invading army is advancing from the east, and everyone knows that the 'winter thunder' can only be the distant rumbling of guns. In a detailed and quietly realistic exposition the village community comes to life. The everyday human problems are overshadowed by foreboding of the unknown—the long-suffered interference of the unpopular régime is about to crumble, but what new terror is to be expected in its place? The central section consists of the diary of a Lutheran pastor who left Berlin in September 1944 to take over the care of this village. Deep in the concerns of his heart is the problem of suicide and divine grace; by the Wannsee he visits the grave of the dramatist Kleist and that of a younger man than himself, a gifted poet of the Lutheran faith who together with his family took his life in 1942; the novel contains quotations from the poetry of Jochen Klepper, and is dedicated in part to his memory. The work moves slowly, but the whole is convincing. We are not presented with any obvious catastrophe. At the end we are still anxiously waiting in the no man's land of a village where all but a handful of the inhabitants have left to trek westwards and where the Russians' entry is to be expected from one day to the next. There is nothing complacent in the narrator's acceptance of Christianity; with much heart-searching he adumbrates the failings of its servants. His central character, the pastor, ruefully notes: 'The safe stronghold has changed into a comfortable house.' Ihlenfeld's second novel, *Kommt wieder, Menschenkinder* ('Come Back, Children of Man'), 1954, is set in a working-class district in the French sector of Berlin, close to the zonal boundary in the north. There are the dark tenements, the ruined churches, the lively shops and streets and the primary school by the overhead railway. The action takes place between Ascension and Whitsunday of 1951. A boy of nine meets death when a sudden subsidence of the paved surface causes this unexpected accident. A journalist, who has had to face many dangers during the war and as a prisoner of war in Russian hands afterwards, feels moved by the fate of this child to raise in his own mind and to discuss with others the religious and philosophical implications of the presence of suffering and evil in the world of a good Creator. *Gregors vergebliche Reise* ('Gregor's Useless Journey'), 1962, examines relationships between the differing nationalities in a rural area that was formerly German and is now part of Poland. The form of the novel is that of an interrogation; Walter Wilhelm Gregor, a German now in his early sixties, has had to interrupt his train journey in order to be questioned by a Polish official at the frontier. Asked about his past, Gregor can recall memories of personal relationships from the time of the First World War onwards. The recurrence of incidents involving violence, particularly in the later career of Dieter Sandberg, a childhood companion who subsequently put his medical knowledge to criminal use under National Socialism, presents Gregor with a challenge in his interpretation of his own memories. The narrator's point of view is by no means unsympathetic to the questioning official, and the attitude of both of them is supplemented by memories written by Gregor's sister, who has since died. They are seeking through fuller understanding an approach to reconciliation.

Wolfgang Borchert (1921–47) wrote with sensitivity, but without nostalgic regrets for a possibly gentler world that was no longer there; indeed, the memory of his generation could scarcely recall a time when Germany was not in a state of crisis or confusion. Borchert's quick febrile style with its bold imagery and colloquialisms that readily acquire poetic significance, could be indicative of a younger generation that wished to call for the brotherhood of man. Apart from the play *Draußen vor der Tür* (English translation published as *The Man Outside*), 1947, Borchert's main writing consists of short stories and sketches where plot is often a secondary consideration, since the tale will be held together by style and mood. The sketches 'Im Schnee, im sauberen Schnee' ('In the Snow, In the Clean Snow') reflect the bleak hopelessness of the author's experience of the Russian campaign. The story 'Die Hundeblume' relates an episode from prison life; vivid naturalism of description is broken up by the obsessions of the prisoners in the exercise yard and by the yearning and triumph of the protagonist's desire to possess a dandelion growing there. Borchert is a poet of his native city Hamburg; for all his pessimism, he gives expression to a love of life associated with his familiar environment: 'That is the smell of life! Nappies, cabbage, plush sofa, onions, petrol, girls' dreams, glue, substitute coffee, cats, geraniums, Schnaps, motor tyres, lipstick.' The story 'Billbrook' tells of a young Canadian airman who, arriving in Hamburg for the first time, finds that there is a district which has his name, Bill Brook. But after setting off gaily to visit it, he finds miles and miles of desolation and rubble, and is overwhelmed with terror at a reality that is unexpectedly frightening. Borchert's last two years of creative writing while contending with increasing ill-health resulted in work which caught the public imagination, both in Germany and elsewhere, as a new voice that could speak for that time in history.

Weißt Du, warum? (English translation published as *Vain Glory*),
1952, by Dieter Meichsner (born 1928), tells of a senseless attack
against the American occupation troops in May 1945 by a band
of German resisters who are lurking in the Bavarian Alps. The
confusion and cruelty of the situation as it affects a young mind
are the emotional basis of the novel. There are analogies of mood
with Hemingway, for example of *A Farewell to Arms*; the pre-
carious idyll of innocent love, the beauty of the mountains in
spring makes more bitter the revulsion against the condition of a
contemporary nomadic man of action. The rather more diffuse
second novel, *Die Studenten von Berlin* (1954), brings many personages together under the central cover of the fate of Berlin in
the last days of the war and its position as a beleaguered garrison
during the time of the air-lift. The life of the battered and divided
city is reflected in particular through the student community of the
Free University established in Berlin in the course of the novel's
action.

Luise Rinser (born 1911) has more than once taken a strong
woman-character as the centre for a novel. *Mitte des Lebens*
('Middle of Life'), 1950, is a love-story that has something of the
fire and vitality of D. H. Lawrence's writing. The heroine, Nina,
has taken part in underground activity against the Nazi régime,
has been imprisoned, has achieved some success as a writer after
1945, and, as her sister takes leaves of her, is on her way to take up
work with an English family. But these events are only peripheral
to a character whose mainspring of being lies in her passionate
and restless personal relations. Her portrait is shown to us largely
through the eyes of an older man who has loved her long and
intensely. In a sequel, *Abenteuer der Tugend* ('Adventure of Virtue'),
1957, Nina's life is followed from 1950 to 1956. She is persuaded
to return from England and to marry a singer, Maurice, with
whom she had previously had a relationship. Her determination
to make this marriage a success meets with serious challenges in
Maurice's temperament, particularly after he has been maliciously
led into heavy drinking by an earlier acquaintance. His death
comes at a time when Nina has found religious faith. The novel

is related entirely in the form of letters sent by Nina to various correspondents. The reader is thus presented with a consistently direct insight into the heroine's viewpoint, whereas in *Mitte des Lebens* she remained a more elusive and enigmatic figure. The two works have subsequently been reissued together, with the title *Nina*. The heroine of *Daniela* (1953) leaves her comfortable middle-class background in order to take up practical social work in a forlorn and poverty-stricken community whose living depends on the peat from the moorlands. The story of Daniela's rehabilitation of these people forms the major part of the narrative. The heroine's relationship with the village priest occasions an unexpected and not altogether convincing conclusion to the novel. *Der Sündenbock* ('The Scapegoat'), 1955, depicts the complexities of two women's impact upon each other, a young woman and her great-aunt. The shorter tale *Jan Lobel aus Warschau* (1948) is quietly told and effective in its tension and atmosphere. The arrival of a homeless and hunted Polish Jew in an Upper Bavarian village shortly before the end of the war brings problems of an emotional character to the market-gardening household which gives him refuge. These writings of Luise Rinser are concerned primarily with personal relationships, frequently showing an acute awareness of emotional issues from a woman's point of view.

Rudolf Krämer-Badoni (born 1913) wrote a satirical novel *In der großen Drift* (1949) which, in first-person narrative, relates the story of a man who begins in an obscure way in the early 1930s, is buffeted about by circumstances and ideas in his student days, finds himself in the army without quite knowing how he got there, becomes a war-hero in Russia and is presented to Hitler, again without any ambition on his own part for such distinction, and when it is all over finds himself clearing bomb-damage from the streets of Frankfurt. The central figure is something of an anti-hero who takes things as he finds them, whose first aim in life is to get by, bitterly sceptical as he is of everything that he considers pretentious or sentimental. *Der arme Reinhold* (1951) has a more lyrical, contemplative touch. Reinhold, nearly sixty, lives as a wood-cutter in a rough shed in the Rhine area and recounts the story of his life; from his lower middle-class home life in Frankfurt he enters the Church, but subsequently his unorthodox behaviour compels him to leave the order, and since then he has been living as an otherworldly pilgrim, taking no thought for the morrow and doing good works as and when the opportunities offer.

Erich Landgrebe (born 1908) takes the war in Russia as setting for his novel *Mit dem Ende beginnt es* (1951), which relates the experiences of a small group of German soldiers and in particular the relationship of one of them with a young Russian woman. The heroine, on hearing that the man who loved her has been killed, comments: 'I can believe that of him. He was like that. Did not know how to live, but could gladly die.' The story is set against the German advance into Russia in the summer of 1941, followed by the retreat through the grey landscape of snow a couple of years later; the historical events which Plievier documents so fully are reflected here on a smaller scale, and there is room for personal emotions to find sensitive expression. Heroic nihilism and a fascinated yearning for death are no solution to the problems and confusions of life, the novel seems to imply. *In sieben Tagen* ('In Seven Days'), 1954, relates the story of a returned prisoner of war who finds the way back to unity with himself only after a long struggle; his wife and children were killed during the war in an air-raid, but he is helped by two women, a mother and a daughter, to regain confidence to face life.

Das geduldige Fleisch (English translation published as *The Willing Flesh*), 1955, by Willi Heinrich (born 1920), is a novel of the war in Russia which is impressive because of the realism and vitality of its material. The characterization is, however, inferior to the deployment of the action and especially the vividness of the scenes. Hans Hellmut Kirst (born 1914) has written in *Null-acht-fünfzehn* (*Zero Eight Fifteen*), 1954-5, a novel that had immediate success. The first volume, describing German barracks life under Hitler in the 1930s, is lively and humorous in a fairly obvious way, with satirical emphasis on relations between a sergeant-major and those under his control.

Eine Stimme hebt an ('A Voice is raised'), 1950, by Gerd Gaiser (born 1908), is about a home-coming soldier who is not so much disillusioned as benumbed by the war and what has followed from it. His wife has been unfaithful to him, and he prefers to go back to the country town where he spent his boyhood. For a time his wounded spirit is silent and unresponsive; but in the chaotic years of 1946 and 1947 he gradually regains a constructive outlook on life. In an atmosphere of bewilderment, apathy, and corruption it is shown how a few people are still capable of heroic self-sacrifice or unspectacular devotion to everyday duties. There are many good descriptions of the living conditions of this time; particularly vivid is that of the townspeople trekking into the countryside to beg, barter, or steal the damson crop in the summer heat. The style recalls the manner of Elisabeth Langgässer; with all its striking qualities it is over-complex, and the blurring of surface reality with archetypal symbols sometimes leads to obscurity. Gaiser's second novel, *Die sterbende Jagd* ('The Dying Squadron', English translation published as *The Falling Leaf*), 1953, follows the experiences of German fighter-pilots and some of those close to them, focusing attention upon a short period during the war when these men come to realize that their task of resisting the attacking squadrons from Great Britain is to lead to defeat, not victory. There is a combination of colloquial language and of a sweet, melancholy and rhapsodic lyricism. The characters are nearly all young people: 'They possessed an intelligence without vocabulary and the ability to be one and the same as their machines.' He shows the knightly code, the sense of exclusiveness, the fatalism and the closeness of death. Vehlgast wonders whether peace in terms of everyday normality is worth looking forward to. Frenssen is resigned to fighting for a cause which he knows is an unworthy one; he considers Hitler as 'the madman', but refuses to think of any alternative to obedience. The diffusion of the interest over the large number of individuals and episodes leads to a certain disjointedness in the narrative, but the general approach is more direct and pithy than in *Eine Stimme hebt an*. *Das Schiff im Berg* ('The Ship in the Mountain'), 1955, in some ways recalls the theme of Broch's *Der Versucher*. The hero of the book is the mountain itself, the changing quality of life on its surface being recounted from prehistorical times; the puny part played by man in this context is emphasized. *Schlußball* (*The Last Dance of the Season*), 1958, looks at life in a fictitious town Neu-Spuhl with reference in particular to its response to the transition from immediate post-war deprivation to commercial prosperity. The social life of a school class of adolescent boys and girls, and to some extent of their families, looks for its seasonal culmination in a ball, to mark the close of a course of dancing lessons. The strands of narrative find their resolution and significance on this particular Saturday night in April. The novel is related in a series of monologues presented by six characters, two men and four women. Soldner, the class-teacher, has sought to instil some appreciation of non-material values in his pupils. But on the night of the ball his approach to Herse Andernoth, mother of one of his pupils, is unsuccessful, and he has to give up teaching. Herse, reluctant to admit that her husband must have died years before, remains a stranger standing apart from the general mood and interests of the townspeople. Apart from Ditta, the girl who succeeds in maintaining some normality in a problematic setting, the speakers of the monologue are solitary; the crippled girl and the dressmaker, and Förckh, the successful business-man whose wife takes her life. A framework is provided by five interludes where voices from another sphere, including that of Soldner's dead wife Rosamund, make their comments. Although Gaiser uses a complicated narrative technique here, his style is more direct than in some others of his works. The lot of women who are deprived of fulfilment and action is sensitively portrayed. *Am Paß Nascondo* (1960) consists of thirteen stories which are linked together by mood, style, landscape, and a number of common characters, as well as by their first-person narrator. The author describes an invented area, with German, Alpine, and Mediterranean features. In a number of the incidents there is a holiday mood, with a savouring of outdoor life, natural beauty, and architectural landmarks from the past. The mysterious and unfriendly land of Calvagory, with its severe restrictions on freedom of movement, is a challenge and a temptation. It is the women figures who can fill the narrator with yearning if they are absent or with inspiration if they are near him—Ness Kämmerer, Lavinia, and his cousin Gepa. Memories and present experience interweave with hallucinations and dream-states, and the living with the dead. When the barges to Monastir glide along 'it is, as if the whole weight, the incomprehensibility, the ugly, merciless insensibility of the world-process were passing by you.' Gaiser has made a distinctive contribution to post-war imaginative prose, with serious and thoughtful writing that probes specific human situations while seeing in them also underlying historical and symbolic implications.

Arno Schmidt (born 1910) is a satirist, sometimes corrosive in his pessimism and often remarkably effective in conveying visual impressions. He writes in a laconic, concentrated style, with a wide range of allusions from literature and contemporary life. His protagonists are disillusioned and frequently solitary, hopeful of little good to come from society and its institutions. The volume *Leviathan* (1949) contains an acid sketch of a train journey out of Berlin in February 1945. A curiously assorted group of individuals commandeer a locomotive and a carriage, and set off on an illicit journey eastwards, only to meet death. *Brand's Haide* ('Brand's Heath'), 1951, is the account of a disabused ex-soldier who settles down to be a writer in conditions of destitution in 1946. He finds happiness in love, until his mistress deserts him to marry an American. For him there is only slight consolation in her promise to send him food parcels, and he is left in a mood that is, typically enough, 'empty and dull grey'. Schmidt continues his poker-faced, staccato jabbing at the condition of humanity in *Aus dem Leben eines Fauns* (1953). Here is a satire on German urban provincial life in 1939; its destruction by bombing in 1944 was no great loss, is its implication. 'Each writer should grasp the nettle reality, and show us everything', we are told. In *Die Umsiedler* ('The Re-Settlers'), 1953, attention is focused on a group of post-war refugees who are being moved by train from

Lower Saxony in order to be re-settled south of Bingen. For all the frustrations of their situation, the protagonist and his beloved, Katrin, can look forward with some hope to the inception of an idyllic period. *Seelandschaft mit Pocahontas* ('Lake Landscape with Pocahontas'), 1954, centres upon a love-affair in an unpretentious holiday setting. Arno Schmidt's probing imagination ranges also over past and future. *Alexander oder was ist Wahrheit* ('Alexander, or What is Truth?'), 1953, depicts a journey by river to Babylon and a sojourn there which coincides with the death of Alexander the Great. The central figure begins as an admirer of the conquering monarch, but becomes progressively disenchanted, until he is left at the end deprived of his earlier faith. The indirect portrait of Alexander, and the varying attitudes to his personality that are presented, have analogies with more recent aspects of German history. *Kosmas oder Vom Berge des Nordens* ('Kosmas, or Concerning the Mountain of the North'), 1955, set in the year A.D. 541, contains discussion of theological and cosmological controversies. The narrator, the twenty-year-old Lykophron, as a pupil of Eutokios, an intellectual pagan, finds much to criticize in the background of the seventeen-year-old Agraule, daughter of a Christian household which has connections with the imperial court. Lykophron's father and Eutokios have to take flight as refugees, but a happy ending is provided for the young couple. There is much that is delightful, unexpected, and charming in this work. A drastic vision of the future, 'Schwarze Spiegel' (in the volume *Brand's Haide*) realizes the dream with which the protagonist of *Leviathan* was toying, the destruction of the human race. We are presented with a central Europe in 1962 after a war that leaves alive only one man and one woman. It may be a garden of Eden made for two, but there are limitations; it is a tale that incidentally parodies fantasy-world fiction in general. Schmidt takes up a comparable theme, though developing it more extensively, in *Die Gelehrtenrepublik* ('The Republic of Learned Men'), 1957. In the year 2008 an American journalist Charles Henry Winer visits two areas of the world which are inaccessible to the general public. His report is reproduced translated into the now dead language of German. The novel consists of two episodes, Winer's impressions of a reserve in the Arizona desert and his subsequent visit to a floating island in the Pacific Ocean which is an 'International Republic for Artists and Scientists'. In the desert enclosure he encounters centaurs, spiders with human heads, and other creatures that have come into existence as after-effects of nuclear warfare or of experimental breeding. The island ship, which is rigidly divided into Eastern and Western sectors, houses selected distinguished people, who may be subjected to heart and brain transplanting operations or be rendered unconscious for decades for the husbanding of their outstanding personal resources. The narrator's flippant manner gives its own emphasis to the sinister implications of the scenes he visits. Schmidt has worked out for himself an individual style and form. Laconic yet richly varied as is his language, he blends diary jottings with interior monologue into a vehicle that effectively reflects the moods he wishes to express. The limited number of characters and the concentrated sequence of events are character-istic of his chosen form, the 'Kurzroman', as he terms it.

The three novels which Wolfgang Koeppen (born 1906) pub-lished in the early years of the Federal Republic are concentrated and distinctive portrayals of aspects of the social situation of the time, seen with disenchantment. In each work the action takes place within a short space of time and uses interior monologues to reveal the thoughts and feelings of the characters. *Tauben im Gras* ('Pigeons on the Grass'—the author quotes from Gertrude Stein—), 1951, is set in a large South German city (Munich is not men-tioned by name). As the visiting speaker Edwin says at the Amerikahaus when lecturing on 'the western spirit', he sees man as endangered and an object of chance. Apart from the threats of mass instability, individuals face insecurity from the person closest to them as well as from their own psychological problems. The marriage of Phillip, a writer who suffers from a sense of pro-fessional inadequacy, with Emilia, who looks back to earlier days of family wealth and resents the present, is on the verge of break-down. Carla wishes to terminate her pregnancy, but Washington

Price, her American coloured lover, hopes to marry her, looking forward to a world where racial prejudice will be overcome. Other episodes also reflect tensions between past and present Germany, or the barriers caused by unawareness in human relationships. In *Das Treibhaus* ('The Hot-House'), 1953, Koeppen takes as his setting the Federal capital Bonn, though providing a somewhat less vivid evocation of an urban environment than in *Tauben im Gras*. The emphasis now lies more upon the point of view of one figure, the parliamentary representative Keetenheuve, who fails to find any positive solution to the problems that haunt him. Having been a refugee, largely in Britain, between 1933 and 1945, he is uneasy in postwar Germany. His political views and his personality contribute to his sense of estrangement from his own party, the opposition, as well as from the governing majority. The recent death of his wife overwhelms him not only with a sense of loss, but also with a feeling of guilt that he had not made a greater effort to make the marriage more successful; a desperate attempt to break out of his emotional isolation only leads to the final catastrophe. The climate of Bonn is that of a hot-house; Federal Germany in the early 1950s is seen as flourishing in an unnatural atmosphere. *Der Tod in Rom* (*Death in Rome*), 1954, acknowledges with an initial quotation its possession of affinity with Thomas Mann's *Der Tod in Venedig*. The atmosphere of Rome is presented with a careful interweaving of past tradition and present-day immediacy, a complex challenge to those members of a German family who meet each other unexpectedly there and respond with varying degrees of uneasiness to the city. Judejahn, now military adviser to an Arab state and designated as a war-criminal in his home country, feels vulnerable and unprotected in a milieu which he formerly visited as a triumphant Nazi commander. His brother-in-law Pfaffrath has been successfully opportunist both before 1945 and during the setting up of the Federal Republic. Both men are alienated from the younger generation as represented by Siegfried, the modernist composer, and by Adolf, his less tortured cousin, a novitiate to the priesthood. The presentation of the points of view of these and other characters is the main narrative method. Though the motivation of the final stages of the action is somewhat unconvincing, the style throughout is rich and precise. The author presents a melancholy picture of his worlds, which are seen with critical sharpness and a consciousness of how far they fall short of the ideal.

5 'If our small example were to keep guard. . .' (Meinrad Inglin)

SWITZERLAND'S policy of democratic neutrality has been maintained through the turmoils of the two twentieth-century European wars. In his essay 'Europäische Schweiz' ('European Switzerland', 1961; based on a lecture given in 1948) Fritz Ernst writes of the satisfaction a Swiss may derive when he looks back over the last 150 years of his history:

Without winning or losing a foot of land the Swiss Confederation has more than doubled its population since 1815, has revised its constitution twice and its legislation continually, has brought its members through commerce ever closer to one another, has indefatigably increased the number of its schools of all kinds, has developed a considerable industry and attained a prosperity that was not deemed possible previously.

With German, French, and Italian as officially recognized languages, its national individuality has never depended on any narrow racial or linguistic bonds. Although an immediate neighbour of Germany and Austria, Switzerland has been an observer of the violent changes and upheavals experienced by these countries, but has itself remained apart from them and retained a consistency in its social life which other countries have often envied. Switzerland's cultural concerns have been both local and internationally orientated. Something of this is observable in the work of two authors who were writing already in the early years of the present century, Hermann Hesse and Robert Walser.

Meinrad Inglin (born 1893) wrote in *Der Schweizerspiegel* ('The Swiss Mirror'), 1938; new version, 1955, a family saga and a picture of Swiss society from 1912 to 1918. If Hesse and Robert Walser frequently offer a mood of rebelliousness against the sober routine of middle-class life, Inglin's novel gives every appearance of reflecting attitudes that would have been characteristic of the majority of Swiss people at the time of the First World War. Colonel Ammann, a member of the national assembly, is discreet and responsible in his participation in committees that make decisions of national significance. His two elder sons take differing points of view; Severin is an admirer of Imperial Germany, while Paul is more sympathetic to French republicanism. Towards the close of the novel strike activities in Swiss towns and the example of the Russian Revolution appear as a threat to Swiss stability. Severin begins to organize a right-wing anti-revolutionary movement, whereas Paul feels impelled to dissociate his own socialist convictions from the outlook of those who wish to overthrow Swiss governmental traditions. The third son, Fred, who finds farming more congenial than study, is prepared to accept the general shape of society as he finds it, and is open to the teaching of his relative René Junod that 'our federal state is therefore predominantly a work of reason, insight, tolerance, a work of the mind', and that 'it would be fine, if our small example were to keep guard over the thought of the possibility of a European union.' Gertrud, sister to the three Ammann sons, leaves her husband Hartmann, a professional army-officer, after discovering her affinities with Paul's friend Albin Pfister, a poet who loses his life in the influenza epidemic of 1918. Inglin's collection of tales *Die Lawine* ('The Avalanche'), 1947, further illustrates the careful, weighty style of his writing. The puniness of man, in the twentieth century as well as in any other age, before the elemental furies of the mountains is the theme of the story which gives the title to this collection and also of the stark 'Drei Männer im Schneesturm'. *Werner Amberg* (1949) is a *Bildungsroman* with a probably autobiographical basis. The first-person narrative traces episodes during childhood and youth in a German-Swiss village. The work concludes with the young man's resolve to leave his work as a hotel-waiter in order to pursue academic studies. Werner Amberg grows up in a family and community atmosphere which is demanding, and at times almost severe, though not without its pointers to a wider, more carefree approach. The supervention of death and disasters in his immediate environment, however, develop in him the conviction that his response must be to endeavour to stand firm against outward misfortunes and to overcome inward fears. Meinrad Inglin has continued in the tradition of solid, three-dimensional realism combined with a sense of service to the community which is characteristic of the two major Swiss novelists of the nineteenth century, Gotthelf and Keller.

Alfred Kübler (born 1890) published in 1939 a collection of short stories *Das Herz—Die Ecke—Der Esel* ('The Heart, the Corner, the Donkey') which show with their deprecatory irony his affinity with the humorous vein of Keller's writing. His major work is the novel of individual development *Öppi* ('Someone'), which appeared in three volumes between 1943 and 1951. With its setting in Switzerland in the early years of the present century, this novel gives a careful reconstruction of the atmosphere of a now irrevocably bygone age that reminds us of Max René Hesse's *Dietrich Kattenburg* or Carossa's autobiography. The loss of his mother when he is twelve is the psychological bruise which is to affect the development of the boy Öppi from that time onwards. He is one of a large family, and his father, innkeeper and timber-merchant in a small village, goes about his own busy and upright life content to leave the youngest child alone, provided he does not get in his father's way. But the boy feels starved of affection, without fully realizing that this is the case, and without being able to find a satisfactory alternative to the maternal warmth he misses. Through this he is alienated from his family, and when he goes to the Gymnasium to embark on a classical education he is further separated from the non-intellectual community life of the village. He has risen above his family and village by taking up an academic education, but always remains mistrustful of much that middle-class urban education stands for. Caught in this social dilemma, he responds by identifying himself with village activities and seeking, for instance, in the local gymnastic club a sense of community which he misses in the town school. Aroused to enthusiasm for science by his headmaster, Öppi becomes, in the second volume of the saga, a student of geology at a university town which is presumably Zürich. The crisis in Öppi's student life occurs after he has taken a term off to visit Italy; dissatisfied with the field of study he has been pursuing so far, he abandons geology to take up art. The situation resembles that of Keller's 'Green Heinrich' in Munich; but in Kübler's novel it is not art but science which proves to be the false vocation. The war of 1914–18 presents another dilemma; although the world outside is caught up in a chaos of tension and catastrophe, he as a Swiss can choose to remain apart. His own slow development is allowed to take its course. He tries drawing and sculpture, only to turn away in order to seek a career as an actor. The third volume centres upon his love affair with Eva, a woman from North Germany, who awakens Öppi to emotional maturity. At this point the novel ends. Öppi is still hesitating, having achieved little or nothing in the way of outward success; but he has become a full man, in the sense which the traditional *Bildungsroman* likes to emphasize. The dilettantism has not been for nothing, we are given to understand; the apprenticeship is over, though the mastery remains a matter for the future. Kübler's unfolding of the story of his hero is slow and sure, indeed there is an absence of a sprightly or ironical approach towards the material. With its large panorama of life in village and town, the work gives an impressively comprehensive picture of Swiss society a generation or so ago.

Kurt Guggenheim (born 1896) has also tackled the psychological problems brought about by life in a small, stable community which has little room for outsiders. His novel *Der Friede des Herzens* ('Peace of Heart'), 1956, takes as its hero a middle-aged man who has always been painstaking and quietly conscientious in the routine of the insurance office which fills up his working hours, and devoted in his leisure time to his wife, daughter, and respectable flat. He attempts to break through the frustrations of the planned prosperity which encloses him on all sides, but fails. His rebellion brings disaster to the woman who becomes his mistress, while he himself, even if only obliquely hurt, has inner conflicts to wrestle with before he finally becomes reconciled to the outward sameness of his life.

The three tales of Hans Walter, *Im Verborgenen* ('On the Quiet'), 1950, depict the surface banality of small-town or village settings, an asphyxiatingly unruffled social background which exacerbates suspicions and latent tensions until tragedy is imminent. Carl J. Burckhardt's volume of *Drei Erzählungen* (1952) contains two stories which link Swiss background and reactions to the indirect impact of the last war. Burckhardt has an urbanity of style and a quiet, human sympathy which gives his stories an attractive smoothness of finish; they are at once regional and universal in scope. His personal friendship with Hugo von Hofmannsthal is recorded in their correspondence during the years from 1919 to the older man's death (*Hugo von Hofmannsthal, Carl J. Burckhardt: Briefwechsel*, 1956). Burckhardt speaks here for Swiss civilization in terms which are comparable to the way in which Hofmannsthal became a representative figure of Austrian culture during those years. Hofmannsthal expresses his fears that with the disappearance of the old order bleak chaos alone will supervene, while Burckhardt refuses to despair of the combined tradition of Christianity and classical humanism. In a letter of August 1928 Hofmannsthal writes: 'I have missed your company too much this whole year—the climate of your mind which is so related and so beneficial to mine. Something very deep is common to us, this urge to grasp all and to conserve—but around this deepest point there is still an infinite sense of companionship.' The Austrian goes on to recount in this context the deep impression that the reading of Gotthelf's tale 'Der Sonntag des Großvaters' has made upon him.

The two contemporary German-Swiss authors who have become best known outside their own country are Friedrich Dürrenmatt (born 1921) and Max Frisch (born 1911). Both are distinguished playwrights. For Dürrenmatt drama has, up to now, been the major preoccupation, whereas fiction has taken a subordinate position, though this does not mean that his imaginative prose has not had a wide appeal. In the case of Frisch the balance of drama and fiction is perhaps more even. The works of both authors see Switzerland in the context of Europe after 1945, and from points of view which, while each one is individual and distinct, have much in common with the West German authors of the 'Gruppe 47'. With his short story *Der Tunnel* (1952) Dürrenmatt quickly and powerfully depicts a threat of chaos and destruction and the way most people would wish to ignore it. *Die Panne* ('The Breakdown', English translation published as *The Dangerous Game*), 1956, demonstrates the way an apparently chance event, a car breakdown, can involve an individual in a strange game that he comes to see not as a way of killing time but as a fateful judgement upon himself. *Grieche sucht Griechin* ('Greek Gentleman Looks for Greek Lady', English translation *Once a Greek . . .*), 1955, shows how the narrow monotony of Archilochos's life is transformed by his marriage with the beautiful Chloé Saloniki, and then confused by his discovery that she has been a courtesan with influence in industry and government.

The title of Dürrenmatt's first detective novel, *Der Richter und sein Henker* (*The Judge and his Hangman*), 1952, indicates themes which have played a paramount part in the author's drama as well as in his fiction—judgement and execution. Bärlach, attached to the police of the city of Berne, although considered by some to be old-fashioned, eccentric and no longer efficient, succeeds in bringing to book an international criminal and also in dealing effectively with the man who murdered a junior member of the police force. In *Der Verdacht* ('Suspicion', English translation published as *The Quarry*), 1953, Bärlach deliberately puts himself in the hands of a surgeon whom he correctly suspects of having been involved in criminal practices in Nazi Germany: '"We think: Emmenberger compels his patients, with the methods that he learned in Stutthof concentration camp, to bequeath their wealth to him, and he kills them afterwards."' In this case Bärlach has to depend upon outside aid in order to escape death; the forces of evil appear to be insurmountably powerful. *Das Versprechen* (*The Pledge*), 1958, by its subtitle 'a requiem to the crime novel', seems to infer that it marks an end to this type of fiction, at least as far as Dürrenmatt is concerned. If in the two earlier detective stories, the author had indicated that a seemingly limited Swiss environment could open up avenues to large-scale international crime, *Das Versprechen* confines itself to a circle of events that remains local and personal. The murder of a child causes a middle-aged police officer Matthäi to devote himself with obsessive single-mindedness to the unravelling of this one case, until his career and his whole earlier way of life have been irrevocably lost. Evil, having moved with the grotesque absurdity of chance, has defeated Matthäi, who did not recognize that 'our reason lights up the world only in a makeshift manner'. *Das Versprechen*, set against a background that is tersely realistic, and narrated with a skilful framework technique, is a psychological study of considerable insight.

Max Frisch's novel *Stiller* (English translation published as *I'm not Stiller*), 1954, is concerned in the first place with the relationship of a complicated individual to those with whom his life has been bound; the broader theme, a critique of mid-twentieth-century civilization from a Swiss point of view, is built up by inference and satirical incident. The conventions of a society that knows that it is reasoned, sensible, economically sound, and traditionally democratic make Stiller rebel against the pre-arranged pattern of career and family. But he is not Promethean in his defiance. As a sculptor he was undistinguished, and he has no inclination to exploit his talents for commercial success. His preliminary breaking-loose as a volunteer in the Spanish Civil War has led to a further lack of faith in himself as well as in the cause which he wished to defend. His marriage to Julika, for a time a promising ballerina, leads to misunderstandings and jealousy of her success, and breaks down. He disappears to America, where he lives for six years, nomadic and at times near suicide, but at least, the implication is, in places where life can be raw and unpredictable. While travelling through Switzerland as a Mr. White from the United States, Stiller is arrested by police authorities who conscientiously set about proving that he is the person whose identity he rejects. His dentist can demonstrate his identity from the state of his teeth, the army authorities deplore the shocking state of his military equipment after six years' neglect, while there is a suspicion that he has had connections with Russian espionage. The court of inquiry decides that he is Stiller, whether he likes it or not, and makes him pay a carefully and fairly calculated fine to cover the expense and trouble that he has caused the authorities. While there is much comedy in the opening sections of the novel, the account of the reconciliation between Julika and Stiller and of their life together by the Lake of Geneva, until Julika's death from tuberculosis, is dominated by a sense of hopelessness and inevitability. At one point Stiller asks himself if his personality and his experiences are real, or to what extent they are second-hand. Does he know Spain through Hemingway, Mexico through Graham Greene, Paris through Ernst Jünger, and so on? And what else has he got from Kafka and Thomas Mann? Frisch's *Stiller* is fluent and apposite in its writing, aware of international trends of thought and life and at the same time specifically Swiss.

In *Homo Faber* (1957) too Frisch centres his attention upon a hero who is beset by the issues of fate and chance, and of the place of the individual in the context of a problematic world. Walter Faber has, it seems, left his Swiss origins and early years behind him. As an engineer engaged in projects in under-developed countries under international auspices, he can see himself as a citizen of the world. The first-person narrative introduces him as a trans-continental air-traveller for whom exotic locations can have few surprises, or seldom surprises that arouse his enthusiasm. He writes colloquially and directly, but is able to conjure up pictures of varied environments with great aptness and to rise to sensitive poetry. Faber insists on looking at the world as a vast mechanism, to be approached with coolness and absence of feeling. His conception of the technologist excludes personal relationships that make emotional demands upon him. If man's security requires him to combat and overcome nature by engineering projects, it will also entail the resistance of nature's inroads upon himself, whether through emotional commitment to others or through the undermining of his physique by disease. At the age of fifty Faber finds that the carefully constructed personality in which he has encased himself is disintegrated, through his close involvement with Sabeth and through the malignancy of his illness. As a young man Faber had not married Hanna when she was pregnant with his child; the marriage might have taken place, and it was a matter of 'chance' again that it did not. That he should fall in love with his own daughter, that she should meet her death by mischance shortly before arriving at her mother's home in Athens, is an ironic and stark recalling, in varied form, of the misunderstandings of the first relationship with Hanna. Max Frisch succeeds in this work in giving a sense of totality within a concise narrative framework. Whether in Central America or New York, in Western Europe or Greece, Walter Faber encounters deep emotional challenges within the space of a few weeks. He has seen so much, but has been so unseeing and mistaken at the same time, that he becomes a moving and tragic figure.

Mein Name sei Gantenbein ('Let my Name be Gantenbein', English translation published as *A Wilderness of Mirrors*), 1964, pursues the problem of individual identity with teasing subtlety, associating the elusiveness of personality with the threatened collapse of the traditional novel form. Rather like the imaginative writer in Jens's *Herr Meister*, who attempts to find an appropriate setting for his central figure and presents his correspondent with various alternatives, the author or narrator thinks of characters— two dominating ones, Gantenbein and Enderlin—and fits stories on to them. 'I try on stories like clothes'; a life needs such stories, as the naked Enderlin needs clothes in the busy streets of the city. Nevertheless, 'every story is an invention . . . every ego that speaks out is a role': 'Sooner or later everyone invents for himself a story which he takes to be his life . . . or a whole series of stories.' It is part of the problem of modern life that it makes stories about individual personalities seem irrelevant, 'and yet human life fulfils itself or fails, in the context of the individual self, and nowhere else.' Gantenbein pretends to be blind, is almost run over by Camilla Huber, tells her stories while she manicures him, and might have been a key-witness at the trial that follows her murder. Or Gantenbein marries a star actress, Lila; alternative and contrasting reactions on her part to the news that he can see are provided. Or Lila is married to an architect, Svoboda, and her lover is Enderlin. The latter, at the age of forty-one, has the offer of an academic post in America, but is reluctant to take it up. Through mischance he suspects that he has only one more year to live; will he live to old age, or will he collapse while starting his car one night? The themes of jealousy and of blindness in love are interwoven. If Switzerland is firmly central, there is an underlying restlessness in the episodes in Jerusalem, Paris, or Berlin, but Peru is a land of hope. At the beginning and towards the close death is in the foreground. The mysterious corpse in the river at Zürich almost succeeds in 'swimming away without a story', but out of the graves the narrator returns to the September sunlight: 'thirst, then hunger, I like life—'.

6 'Reality is a task...' (Heinrich Böll)

A FORTNIGHTLY journal, *Der Ruf* ('The Call'), was founded in the summer of 1946 in Munich by Hans Werner Richter and Alfred Andersch. In April 1947 it was forbidden by the authorities of the military government. Some months later Richter invited a number of colleagues to a meeting to discuss the launching of a new journal, but the publication of this periodical too was forbidden. The meeting that took place was the first one of the 'Gruppe 47', and these meetings, where individual authors read from their writings to make them available for group criticism, took place regularly once, and for a time twice, yearly. Hans Werner Richter continued to be the guiding spirit of these gatherings, and Reinhard Lettau, who has provided detailed documentation of the Group, wrote in 1967 that he 'cannot imagine the happy development of German literature after the war without the work of this man.'[1] The group aimed to encourage new authors, not those already known, and the average age of those who attended was between twenty and forty. There was an absence of any narrow doctrine, which was seen as an advantage, and it was claimed that the Group was free from political or religious commitment.[2] There was opposition to extreme subjectivism, to 'meaningless metaphor' and 'associative stammering': 'One does not wish to prescribe to the author what he has to write. One does not ask "What are you writing?", but "How are you writing?" Writing, it was said, begins with the control of the element of craftsmanship, the medium of language ... The aim is communication in a form which has been aesthetically mastered.'[3] There was an avoidance of 'all too abstract

1 Reinhard Lettau (ed.), *Die Gruppe 47. Bericht, Kritik, Polemik*, Neuwied und Berlin, 1967, p. 17.

2 Heinz Friedrich, *Hessische Nachrichten*, 22.9.1948, and A. Wiss-Verdier, *Documents* (Paris), September/October 1949, quoted by Lettau, op. cit.

3 Arnold Bauer, *Die Neue Zeitung* (Munich), 11.5.1949, quoted by Lettau.

discussions'.[4] By 1957 the Group had become an institution, and most of those who had attended ten years earlier were 'no longer the poor poets from the garrets of the first post-war period'.[5] In 1961 some influential members of the Group intervened in West German politics on behalf of the Social Democratic Party. The tone of the criticism at sessions was sharp, and could have decisive effects on the author's hopes for publication.[6] Hermann Kesten believed that German literature would not look different, if there had never been a 'Gruppe 47', but that the cultural-political situation in the Federal Republic would be poorer without the Group.[7] Rolf Schröers indicated that the 'Gruppe 47' did not work through any tangibly official pronouncements but rather through a group atmosphere. In the earlier years, then unknown authors had to face considerable difficulties; the German public wanted time to get to know works by Thomas Mann, Hesse, and Kafka, or by figures of international repute from outside Germany such as Hemingway, before they were willing to explore the possibilities offered by new writers. Later the situation changed; the Group 'became famous through its members who had become famous.' Older authors continued not to be admitted to the sessions, and those who were permitted to attend came as guests of H. W. Richter.[8] In the same year Heinrich Böll maintained that the Group's influence was insignificant up to 1955, 'that is, in the decisive years after the end of the war', and that ten years later it had remained what it was: '. . . an instrument of publication, a forum, a medium, naturally a market as well; and it still consists of Hans Werner Richter plus the unknown—its mythical character is unmistakable. It is there and yet impalpable, one can't get hold of it.'[9]

Richter has made most impression as a creative writer by novels

4 Martin Walser, *Radio Bern*, November 1952, quoted by Lettau.

5 *Die Gegenwart*, (Frankfurt), 5.10.1957, quoted by Lettau.

6 *Der Spiegel* (Hamburg), 24.10.1962, quoted by Lettau.

7 Hermann Kesten, *Deutsche Zeitung* (Cologne), 13/14.7.1963, quoted by Lettau.

8 Rolf Schröers, *Merkur* (Cologne and Berlin), May 1965, quoted by Lettau.

9 Heinrich Böll, *Merkur* (Cologne and Berlin), August 1965, quoted by Lettau.

published during the early years of the 'Gruppe 47'. His professional manner is already evident in his first novel *Die Geschlagenen* ('The Defeated,' published in English as *The Odds Against Us*), 1949, a documentary-style story of defeat and imprisonment. *Sie fielen aus Gottes Hand* (*They Fell From God's Hand*), 1951, is a large-scale novel which recounts the adventures of a dozen characters from the eve of the invasion of Poland, September 1939, to a day in 1950 when they are all collected in a camp for displaced persons in Germany. None of these figures is German by birth—there are men and women from the Baltic lands, Poland, and Russia, from the Balkans, from Luxemburg, France, or Spain—but all of them are bound up in their separate way with the fate of Germany. The author seldom commits himself to comment on their fortunes; he prefers to report, and we are told that the material for his characters and plots was based on a factual investigation of individual cases. His sympathies are with the helpless individual, of whatever nationality he may be, who is exposed to the bewildering, incalculable chances of war and its subsequent confusion. Richter handles his large cast with skill, and sketches in the rapidly changing scenes with adroitness, for we are not limited to Central Europe, but are transported to America, Africa, Israel, and Vietnam. The net is cast widely, and it is not surprising that the deeper aspects of human experience sometimes elude the author. Richter employs a similar method in the novel *Du sollst nicht töten* ('Thou Shalt not Kill'), 1955. The ground covered is the war, from its outbreak to its finish, the episodes being located far and wide throughout Europe. What unity there is in this panorama is provided by family ties. Of the three Lorenz brothers, one is a supporter of Nazism, another is opposed to its outlook, while a third attempts to make his way through the war years without becoming implicated in political issues. The fates of their sister Helene and of Jürgen Schiemann, who is in love with her, are further strands in the narrative. There is much that is challenging and tragic in this novel.

Walter Jens (born 1923), who has been active in literary criticism as well as creative writing, is less concerned in his novel about the future with the more speculative issues that Hesse, Kasack or Werfel discuss in their contributions to this type of writing. *Nein. Die Welt der Angeklagten* ('No. The World of the Accused'), 1950, is more specifically directed to the problems of individual liberty in a menacing future. The world-state has divided mankind into three classes—judges, witnesses, and plaintiffs; it is run by a police system that minimizes man's capacities of independent thought or unselfish impulse. The work may be compared with Orwell's *1984* or Kafka's *Der Prozeß*. Jens's subsequent novel *Der Blinde* (*The Blind Man*), 1951, describes the reactions of a man in middle life who finds himself confronted by sudden blindness. The novel *Vergessene Gesichter* ('Forgotten Faces'), 1952, is concerned with the inmates of a home for retired actors. The Maison Savarin has a long tradition as a refuge for elderly people with stage connections, but the local municipality wishes to convert the chateau into a hotel and museum. A small group of old people finally have to take the long train journey to Paris and alternative accommodation. The novel presents episodes of humour and pathos, with sensitive insight into the discrepancy between present and past, possible and impossible, in this unusual community. *Der Mann, der nicht alt werden wollte* ('The Man who did not want to grow old'), 1955, links up the theme of old age with a German academic setting; a retired university professor investigates the motives underlying the suicide of one of his former students. *Herr Meister* (1963), a 'dialogue about a novel', consists of an exchange of letters between an imaginative writer and a literary historian. The former presents plans for a new novel, beginning with the wish to show the impact of dictatorship in a German university town in 1933. In the ensuing correspondence alternative suggestions are sketched out, and are accompanied by critical comments which probe into problems of the contemporary novelist. For the imaginative writer, in this final letter, feels unwilling to give up the novel form for the sake of essay, sketch, or lyrical meditation, as his friend suggests; however, the approach to the novel which is right for him, which is compelling and committing, has yet to be found, and the search is to go on.

The novel *Die größere Hoffnung* ('The Greater Hope'), 1948, by Ilse Aichinger, who was born in 1921 in Vienna, relates in lyrical, stylized manner the fate of a partly Jewish girl from the time when, as an eight-year-old child, she is separated from her mother who has to flee before the German invaders of Austria in 1938, to the day near the end of the war when she meets her death from a stray shot during the street-fighting in Vienna in 1945. There is much that is poignant in this novel—the group of little waifs who have nowhere to play together except the dilapidated cemetery, or the description of the forced labour conditions in a wartime factory. Ilse Aichinger has achieved a greater formal precision in her collection of short stories *Der Gefesselte* (*The Bound Man*), 1953, with their imaginative treatment of the symbolic content of a world underlying the reality of everyday life.

Alfred Andersch (born 1914) grew up in Munich and was interned in Dachau concentration camp for six months in 1933 as a result of his Communist affiliations at the time. Subsequently he was an industrial worker, and then became part of the German army, from which he deserted on 6 June 1944 in Italy. His auto-biographical 'account' *Die Kirschen der Freiheit* ('The Cherries of Freedom'), 1952, traces an inner development as well as giving a succinct and graphic picture of the environment of his childhood and youth. His earlier life is seen as a preparation for the central decision of separating himself from the group where he finds himself in 1944; the culminating purpose of his writing the account is to describe one single moment of freedom. Such moments, he writes, are precious and rare; to escape from society is to free oneself from fate, if only for a brief interlude. He has detached himself from the determinism of Marxism, or indeed from any movement depending upon collective attachment, asserting that he can only be committed to his personal experience and vision.

Like the autobiographical account, the novel *Sansibar oder der letzte Grund* ('Zanzibar, or the Last Reason', published as *Flight to Afar*), 1957, is tautly and economically written. In the earlier work the author had referred to the 'neo-realism' of some immediate post-war films as a style that he found sympathetic; his first novel conjures up the atmosphere of a small German town on the Baltic coast in 1937 with both restraint and poetry. The conception of freedom worked out in the autobiography is demonstrated here in the lives of five people; a situation is shown in which there is the call to co-operation as well as that to individual liberty. In *Die Kirschen der Freiheit* oppressive compulsion is followed by a brief period of anarchic self-realization, after which must come reorientation in a social order which is preferable to the first one, but none the less contains features of routine and restriction that are disillusioning. A comparable pattern can be traced in *Sansibar*; in the process of escape from or defiance of National Socialist society, the climax of flight brings a short-lived interlude of liberating enthusiasm, to be followed by the return home, or by a new stability in a different and preferable environment, or by death. For the brief time of their action together, less than twenty-four hours, the five characters form themselves into a charismatic community separate from the large-scale organizations that otherwise dominate their lives. Andersch gives as motto to the novel some lines by Dylan Thomas, concluding with:

> Split all ends up they shan't crack;
> And death shall have no dominion.

The boy experiences an inward transformation, the fisherman Knudsen has the satisfaction of a task well done, while Judith, the Jewish young woman who needs to be rescued in her flight, has less choice in her part of the enterprise than the other four characters. Gregor, the representative of the Communist party organization, and the Protestant priest Helander are both bound by an overt commitment to organizations which expect conformity to a given interpretation of life. But neither is an orthodox representative of his institution; both are involved in crises of faith which make them doubt the effectiveness of their party or church in face of National Socialism. For Gregor it is the experience of beauty, in landscape, in woman, and in a work of art, that acquires a significance not explicable to him in party terms. Helander's form of action takes him outside the order to which he has belonged; he helps to save Knudsen and Gregor by dying in circumstances that are contrary to the beliefs he has earlier stood for.

Die Rote (*The Redhead*), 1960, set in post-war Venice, covers the period of a long week-end. The heroine Franziska makes an impulsive escape from her husband and her lover, both German business-men who have involved her and themselves in a relation-ship from which she feels she must break free. Andersch gives a not unsympathetic portrayal of a German business-man on a visit to France in 'Mit dem Chef nach Chenonceaux', one of the short stories collected in the volume *Geister und Leute* ('Spirits and People', published as *The Night of the Giraffe*), 1958. The newly found liberty brings its anxieties and dangers, but also leads to living experience of a novel kind. Venice is more than the dead end it was for Aschenbach in Thomas Mann's *Der Tod in Venedig*; it is more than an alien environment that contrasts with German or Austrian normality, as it may seem in Goethe's *Venetian Epigrams* or Hofmannsthal's *Andreas*. Venice does indeed lead Franziska close to peril and death. Her encounter with Patrick O'Malley leads her to wonder whether Venice is not a cage in which the Irishman is caught with his enemy Kramer, the former Gestapo officer who is now an influential figure in the criminal underworld of the city. But new life is given to her not by O'Malley, but by Fabio Crepaz, the Italian musician who had formerly been a Communist partisan, until after 1945 he came to the conclusion 'that ideas lost their content, because un-substantial; in their place arose mere power-blocks, the two big nihilistic mechanisms'. She will work in a soap-factory in Mestre and live there with his family until the child she is expecting is born.

'Reality is a task. . . . It requires our active, not our passive attention. What is real *is* fantastic.' These words of Heinrich Böll (born 1917) indicate something of his experience of contemporary life as the first challenge which he has felt the need to take up, particularly in novels, shorter tales, short stories, essays, and radio-drama. The immediacy of Böll's evocation of his world has met with a breadth of response from readers not only within West and East Germany, but also in the non-German, international context, that indicates the high degree of its relevance. His writing has appealed directly to a wide range of readers, while showing itself as fruitful material for the critical analyst of literary texts. By warmly sympathetic characterization of individual figures, especially of those who are lost or frustrated in an indifferent environment, by his humour, whether genial or satirical, in a palpably day-to-day context, or by the sensitivity of his love-stories, where the gentle patience of heroines plays a considerable part, Böll has built up a world where many readers can feel readily at home. At the same time a critical view of various aspects of contemporary society is maintained, with something of the programmatic approach of Diderot in the *drame bourgeois* or Brecht in his epic theatre; in one of his earlier essays ('Bekenntnis zur Trümmerliteratur', 'Avowal to Literature of the Ruins') Böll writes appreciatively of Dickens, with reference to social purpose, humour and warmth of heart. What came before 1933, indeed, before 1939, plays only a small part in the author's imaginative world, though he can look back wonderingly at the Roman and the Roman Catholic monuments of Cologne and the permanence and flux of the Rhine. But for Böll the trauma of the years 1939–45 is a factor of recent history that puts the earlier past a great distance away. After the war came the peace; he recalls the chaos and the starvation amid the ruined towns, the advent of the currency reform, bringing neon-lights and shop-windows for all, and of the 'economic miracle' of the 1950s and the advent of a new generation with no conscious memory of events that were so fundamental to his experience.

His first two novels deal directly with war experiences. *Der Zug war pünktlich* (*The Train was on Time*), 1949, recounts the brief days in a soldier's life in 1943 from the time when he boards a special train in the Ruhr in order to be transported back to the

Eastern front. The train-journey can become a motif to indicate a quality of life, with its suggestion of passivity and helplessness, and Andreas's anticipation of his death in the near future. *Wo warst du, Adam?* (English translation published as *Adam, Where Art Thou?*), 1951, narrates the fate of a group of officers and men who are gradually retreating back to Germany from the Balkans, until Feinhals, the main protagonist, meets his death from German firing, just as he is returning to his home village when it is about to capitulate to American forces. The emphasis on the time-factor and the use of repetition combine to demonstrate the pattern of the narrative, where long, tense periods of waiting are interrupted by episodes of destructive action. Apart from rare moments of love and friendship, or happiness through unexpected impressions given by daily life, the theme of the senselessness of war dominates the outer action, and the sequences of monotony and sudden violence underline this approach. The novel may be criticized as tending to fall apart into separate episodes, or as being too black and white in its approach, but it is full of incident and incisive and varied in its action and characterization.

Und sagte kein einziges Wort ('And said not a single word', English translation published as *Acquainted with the Night*), 1953, and *Haus ohne Hüter* (published as *The Unguarded House*), 1954, were Böll's first novels of family life. In the earlier of these two works a marriage is threatened by the husband Fred's reluctance to live together with his wife Käte and their children in unsatisfactory living conditions. The narrative is presented from the points of view of the husband, who is a telephone operator, and the wife who bears patiently with the grim chores of her immediate environment and struggles to sustain her husband in his disturbed state of mind. Much of *Haus ohne Hüter* is seen from the point of view of two boys on the verge of adolescence who have never known their fathers. Each child recognizes that there is something lacking about his mother; Martin has wealth around him (the family have an interest in a jam factory), but his mother's emotional life has become frozen in the past, while his grandmother's overriding trait is greed for rich food. Martin is, however, more fortunate than his school-friend Heinrich, whose mother is dependent on a succession of 'uncles' to support her and her two children; in Martin's Uncle Albert there is a sense of protective responsibility towards the younger generation, even though it may be frequently thwarted. In this novel the author ingeniously varies the scenes from urban life which he describes, from the glitter of prosperity to the shabbiness of more ordinary scenes. *Das Brot der frühen Jahre* (*The Bread of Our Early Years*), 1955, is Böll's first extended love-story. A young man who specializes in repairs to washing machines falls in love with a young woman from the smaller town where he spent his earlier life. His actions during this fateful Monday are interspersed with flashbacks which explain his present mood in terms of earlier deprivations. As a schoolboy and in the early days of his apprenticeship he was constantly hungry; since then material considerations have played a sobering part in his life, until the encounter with Hedwig brings about sudden overwhelming transformation.

In *Billard um halbzehn* (*Billiards at Half Past Nine*), 1959, Böll has presented a novel that represents the culmination of his writing during the 1950s, offering as it does a wide panorama of time past and present, involving a considerable number of characters and points of view, while at the same time drawing attention closely to happenings and issues centring upon a few hours in the present. The work is highly co-ordinated. The streams of consciousness and monologues of various figures in the course of one day, 6 September 1958, contain references back to emotionally significant events in the past. In three generations of a family of architects the author conjures up historical perspectives more emphatically than in earlier works. Through the eyes of the old man, Heinrich Fähmel, the life of pre-1914 Germany is presented in careful reconstruction, while his son Robert's point of view takes him back to 1935, when he and his friend Schrella demonstrated at school against a Nazi teacher, with consequences that were to be far-reaching in the lives of them both. Robert's son Joseph may have to contend in the future with some unknown equivalent to the misfortunes that older members of the family have had to suffer. The Fähmel family is intrinsically whole and healthy, and given more favourable outward circumstances, might have lived in idyllic serenity. They have, it is true, retained their sense of belonging together, and professional work has ensured stability in material conditions and congeniality of occupation. But these factors are not in themselves sufficient to guarantee the full life when unscrupulous aggressiveness intervenes, as for instance in the First World War and in National Socialism. Hence this apparently favoured family has experienced havoc and waste of life within itself, and the members of the family are aware of the width of the gap that separates each from the other, even though they share common beliefs and tastes. 'Grandfather built the monastery, father blew it up with high-explosive, and Joseph has built it anew.' If Heinrich Fähmel has maintained a fair degree of stability, it has not been without certain deep misgivings at what it has cost; his wife Johanna collapsed under the strain of her sense of indignation against the oppression of 'lambs' by 'buffaloes', whereas his son Robert has become quietly embittered and withdrawn. The first half of the novel consists of exposition, centring upon the Fähmel family. The advent of two men from outside acts as catalyst to the action. Nettlinger, the former Nazi, has lost his earlier dangerousness and is shown humorously as having adapted himself smoothly to the Germany of the 1950s. Schrella, the friend for whom Robert has been waiting for many years, revisits his home-city after an absence of over twenty years, only to move on, as wanderer, after a few hours. The narrative, though using leitmotifs and flash-backs with great subtlety and skill, and sustained by richness of language, is firmly planted within an effectively simple structure.

Ansichten eines Clowns (English translation published as *The Clown*), 1963, is less extensive in its approach than *Billard um halbzehn*. It is a story told by a narrator whose uncompromising indignation is particularly aroused by a group of Catholic middle-class intelligentsia whom he regards as responsible for separating him from the woman he loves, and with whom he has been living for some years. They have not married, partly because he does not share her religious beliefs. Hans Schnier, the clown, arrives in Bonn early one evening, alone and harried by awareness of recent professional disasters; the novel ends a few hours later with his return to the station, this time as a beggar, not a traveller. The action is concentrated into the time which Hans spends in his flat, for the most part alone with his thoughts and memories, and in contact, chiefly over the telephone, with people he knows. The major exception to the telephone dialogue is the visit from his father, but he has long mistrusted his parents' wealthy, industrial background. Thus the protagonist combines an obsessively poignant devotion to a love which is no longer returned with a strong dislike of much that he considers representative of the country in which he lives. To the loss of Marie, in the present, there corresponds the death of Hans's elder sister Henrietta when he was a boy in 1945, the shock of which has fashioned much of his subsequent outlook. The narrator's melancholy and anger suffuse the whole work, where social criticism is incidental to the subjectivity of its inward emotionalism.

The tale *Entfernung von der Truppe* (translation published as *Absent without Leave*), 1964, has as its narrator a man of forty-seven who at the time of writing his reminiscences is about to hand over his wholesale coffee business to his son-in-law. He describes himself as a romantic and a neurotic, and his story as an idyll and a memorial chapel. He is an eccentric, scornful and apathetic perhaps, but not complacent or whimsical. The highlight of his life has been the short-lived happiness with his wife and her family over twenty years earlier. Now memories and family loyalty remain with him, though precariously, after other groups have been cast aside—National Socialism, the churches and the new society of contemporary West Germany.

Heinrich Böll has written a considerable number of non-fictional essays and commentaries which throw further light upon his imaginative writing. The four lectures delivered at the University of Frankfurt during the winter of 1963–4 (*Frankfurter*

Vorlesungen, 1966) argue eloquently for an 'aesthetic of the humane' and from the presupposition that language, love, and commitment are distinctively human factors which define man's position with regard to himself, to other people, and to God. Home, neighbourhood, and family are seen as units favourable to the development of creative writing, in contrast to impersonal organizations; a loss of the sense of neighbourliness and home is seen as one of the features of recent years. He is champion here too of German literature from 1945 to 1954, a period that was rich in 'humane realism', a term that may be found not inapposite as an indication of the texture of his writing.

Satirical wit, sharp and delicate, linked with surrealist fantasy, give the particular tone to *Sternstaub und Sänfte* ('Stardust and Sedan-Chair'), 1953, by Wolfdietrich Schnurre (born 1920). These 'notebooks of the poodle Ali' contain aphoristic comments on life by a professional animal of letters, an account of his day-to-day life with various other non-human creatures. Berlin has become a central theme in Schnurre's writing. *Als Vaters Bart noch rot war* ('When Father's Beard was still Red'), 1958, is a 'novel in stories', a collection of twenty pieces that form a unit in the close relationship of father and son over a period of time that moves from the Weimar Republic to the first years of National Socialism. The author has referred to himself as identifiable with the little Bruno, and it is from his point of view we are shown a realistic, humorous, moving, and at times idyllic picture of a Berlin where Bruno's father found that it was a struggle to make both ends meet and at the same time live in a relatively unrestricted and peaceful manner. The direct style of *Als Vaters Bart noch rot war* is replaced by a more recondite, oblique approach in the 'chronicle' *Das Los unserer Stadt* ('The Fate of Our Town'), 1959. A sequence of episodes involves human beings and animals, and bears a relationship to events from 1945 onwards; the city is occupied by forces representing contrasting ways of life, and after they have departed the state begins to rearm. Public misfortunes include floods, plague, and a shortage of air. A central section of the work, based on material discovered by the narrator, conjures up exotic settings—tropical forests, a mountain that moves, and a hitherto unexplored plateau. Apart from the forms of the short story and the radio-play, Schnurre has expressed himself on current events and on the relationship of literature to life in forthright essays; a number written between 1946 and 1964 are collected in the volume *Schreibtisch unter freiem Himmel* ('Writing Desk under a Free Sky'), 1964.

Wolfgang Hildesheimer (born 1916) has written short stories, such as the title-story of the volume *Ich trage eine Eule nach Athen* ('I carry an Owl to Athens', that is, 'coals to Newcastle'), 1956, which are amusing and sharp, entertaining because of their neat expression of not quite total absurdity. His novel *Tynset* (1965) records the thoughts and actions of a man from bed-time to nine in the morning during an autumn night which promises snow, fog, and the coming of winter. He has left Germany eleven years previously in order to live in the spacious wooden house in Norway which he inherited from a distant relative. In the course of the night he gets up and wanders into various rooms of the house. The one human contact that takes place is with his house-keeper Celestian who, sitting drunk in the kitchen at 2 a.m., is surprised by his entry and at first thinks he is God. The protagonist is caught in a sense of futility and indifference. 'Nowhere, the only place where I can breathe, set free from everything. . . .' He ought to go somewhere, for instance, to Tynset, to which the railway timetable draws his attention. Next morning the church bells inform him that there will be a funeral in the locality. But he will go neither to the funeral nor Tynset; he will probably stay in bed. There are various fantasies and flash-backs in the course of the night, which usually underline the absurd or the horrific. The most developed of these episodes recalls a 'farewell-party' which the protagonist gave, and its interruption by an American evangelist who subsequently dies in his snowbound car. Written with poise and polish, the novel consistently maintains its protagonist's mood of lethargic disenchantment.

Siegfried Lenz (born 1926), in an autobiographical postscript to the collection of stories *Stimmungen der See* ('Moods of the Sea'),

1962, has written of his preoccupation in a number of his novels
and stories with what happens to a man who 'falls', who is losing
in life. He speaks of his variations on 'the theme of the "hero"
who rebels against an inevitable downfall and is overcome'. His
first novel, *Es waren Habichte in der Luft* ('There were Hawks in
the Air'), 1951, follows the fate of a schoolteacher in Finland who
is being hunted by authority for political reasons. Though he
fails to escape, the youth who was once his pupil is able to cross
the frontier. *Duell mit dem Schatten* ('Duel with the Shadow'),
1953, is set in the Libyan desert where a German ex-colonel,
accompanied by his daughter, is revisiting the scene of war-time
experiences that were crucial to him. Their encounter with two
British brothers who share some of the German's background
experiences in this setting leads to a series of unexpected adventures
involving the estrangement of the daughter from her father and
culminating in the latter's death.

Der Mann im Strom ('The Man in the Water'), 1957, centres
upon a professional diver who some little time after the war
obtains work in the salvaging of ships that have been sunk in the
port of Hamburg. With detailed, careful realism Siegfried Lenz
describes life in this milieu, its dangers, its scope for initiative, its
comradeship. Hinrichs comes into conflict with the young man
who pays attentions to his nineteen-year-old daughter, a youth
with some of the less desirable traits of the generation that has
been growing up in the aftermath of war. But Hinrichs is fearful
that his age will be held against him in his work, and his steps
to avoid disqualification eventually lead to his downfall. As he
says: 'I have made a mistake, and this consisted in growing old.
You can only afford this mistake if you are firmly dug in somewhere. But someone, chief, who is old and wants to start afresh,
might as well let himself be thrown on to the scrap heap.' It is a
novel told with sober, unobtrusive quietness, without emotionally
rhetorical tones, but tense in many moments of its action. The
uncertainty of manner in the first two novels has now been
replaced by a greater mastery of narrative methods and characterization. Lenz's next novel, *Brot und Spiele* ('Bread and Circuses'),

1959, is again a study set in a specialized environment which is delineated with meticulous insight, centring upon a character who is fighting a losing battle in a métier that requires unusual qualities and where the competitive spirit is fierce. Bert Buchner, formerly an invincible long-distance runner of international status, is running his last race, facing the competition of younger men. The novel sweeps on in one long paragraph which coincides with the duration of the 10,000 metres race; the narrator is Buchner's friend, who has known him since the war and who first saw how he could run while he was in flight from a prisoner of war camp in the north-west of Schleswig-Holstein. Memories of earlier times together are intercalated with the framework of the present race. Buchner's success has been achieved at the expense of personal friendships and with the assistance of timely un-scrupulousness. The narrator can comment on the champion's rise, which is contemporary with the economic and social changes taking place in post-war Germany; a certain indirect element of social criticism accompanies the description of Buchner's career. Nevertheless, it is defeat and flight that are uppermost in the narrator's mind from the moment the last race starts:

Whatever is he doing? Is that defeat already? Yes, it is announcing its presence already at the start: the certainty of defeat drives him on into this spurt, he does not want to hear the threatening steps of his opponents behind him, nor to feel their burning breath in his neck: Bert takes flight from them, in order to take flight from himself. . . .

With *Stadtgespräch* ('Town Talk'), 1963, Lenz gives an analysis of the complexity of the tensions present in a Norwegian town under German occupation during war-time. The uneasy relation-ship between occupying forces, townspeople, and local resistance-group is continuously present. The reason for the town gossip lies in the shooting of forty-four leading citizens as hostages by the German commandant, and in the query as to whether this event could have been prevented, particularly if Daniel, the young leader of the resistance group, had surrendered to the Germans. As in *Brot und Spiele*, the central character is not presented directly, but as seen through the eyes of someone very close to him; in *Stadtgespräch* the narrator is Tobias Lund, whose father was one of the executed hostages and whose sister is Daniel's beloved. Part of the paradox of the situation is that there is a lack of sympathy between the townspeople and the resistance-group. Both Daniel and the German commandant are leaders of clear, hierarchical systems, and both expect support or obedience from the town. The small resistance-group has voluntarily separated itself from the ordinary citizens; it has set itself apart, and its ascetic dedication may be resented as an assertion of moral superiority. If Tobias and his supporters tend to become discredited as the action proceeds, this is partly due to the personality of the German commandant, who succeeds in separating his enemies although the cause that he represents is hopeless and unjustifiable. Daniel's leadership fails, and after the war he is unable to find reintegration in the local community. Whether finally the period of suffering and decline is over for him and positive content can return into his life in the future, is a question which the author leaves open. *Stadtgespräch* is a serious, subtle treatment of social relationships in a situation of anguished abnormality, presented in terms of understatement and open-minded concern. A sense of pity underlies Lenz's conception of character. The dilemmas posed by chance events and human frailty are never to be underestimated, and if they are to find solution, it will be through reasonableness and good will.

With his first novel *Ehen in Philippsburg* ('Marriages in Philippsburg', English translation published as *The Gadarene Club*), 1957, Martin Walser (born 1927) gave a picture of contemporary social life in a south-west German town. Hans Beumann, a young man who has studied at a nearby university, makes his way by attaching himself to the daughter of a manufacturer of television and radio equipment, though it is not until Anna Volkmann has had an abortion, in a state of great distress, that he feels that he at last loves her. The reader's attention is then directed to the marital problems of two older men, Benrath, a doctor, and Alwin, a man with an interest in practical politics. Thus two separate stories are interpolated before the novel returns to Beumann, with the indication that his coming marriage with Anna may well be jeopardized by the infidelities that are customary in this circle. Criticism of modern urban society and of the world of business is continued in *Halbzeit* ('Half-Time'), 1960, linked again with the theme of the tension between stability and flux in erotic relationships. However, *Halbzeit* is considerably more extended in its range, and its first-person narrator Anselm Kristlein is more complex and dominating in his role in the work than is Hans Beumann in *Ehen in Philippsburg*. As the novel opens he is convalescent from an illness, and soon discovers that his work as a commercial representative has crumbled to nothing. He has a wife, Alissa, and small children, but more of his attention is taken up with his interests in other women. The central episodes of the first section focus upon his friend Josef-Hinrich's party to celebrate his engagement (to his eleventh fiancée). Through another friend Edmund, Anselm obtains entry into a really big firm, that of Frantzke, as a compiler of advertising material; here his stylistic virtuosity can find immediate application. The author again shows his skill in manipulating group scenes in this second section; apart from the business conference, there is the festive day of Frantzke's honorary degree, celebrated by a lunch-party (with workers from a neighbouring building-site looking in), an afternoon at Frantzke's villa and a more select party again in the evening. Anselm's longings for Melitta, whom he remembers from childhood days, bring back scenes from his earlier life, while his pursuit of Susanne, Joseph-Hinrich's fiancée, introduces the background of her earlier wandering life. The third section shows Anselm's preparations for and return from a business-trip to New York, intercalated with episodes indicating, for instance, unusual group activities of local children and of a group of men of the town. There is one more lavish and hectic party, to celebrate the New Year at the Frantzkes', with the consequence that Anselm has to ask for readmission as a hospital patient. *Halbzeit* is rich in material, teeming with incidents and people, yet with a narrator who can be inward-looking and self-critical.

Die Blechtrommel (The Tin Drum), 1959, by Günter Grass (born 1927), had an immediate impact upon critics and readers when it appeared, and it may have been influential in introducing a harsher and more strident note into German literature. Its vitality, imaginative fertility and uncompromising naturalism make their effect if one considers one episode in isolation, or all the more as the slabs of material accumulate in chronological sequence. The first-person narrator Oskar Matzerath, enclosed under supervision in a hospital institution at the age of thirty, writes the story of his life. He presents a series of episodes beginning with an October afternoon in 1899 as it affected his grandmother Anna Bronski, reaching his own birth in 1924, and proceeding through childhood and youth in Danzig to the war years and after, from Danzig to Düsseldorf. There are forebears to the novel in the Bildungsroman and in the Zeitroman of the post-1945 era; the individual development of a hero who sees Goethe and Rasputin as his models takes place against a closely observed background of everyday life, while being affected by public events of the time. Irony and burlesque are predominant, for Oskar looks at the world from his own unique position. His calculated fall down the cellar-steps on his third birthday retards his growth, but not his intellectual alertness, though those around him assume that he is mentally backward. 'I remained the three-year-old, the gnome, Tom Thumb.' Oskar has the ability to shatter glass with his voice, as is discovered when adults attempt to deprive him of his tin-drum. Comedy and fantasy can jar abruptly against horror and grimness. In the episode where Oskar's drum-beating upsets the mood of a Nazi rally the satirical humour is direct; a little later Oskar hopes for a 'little, private miracle' in church, if the boy Jesus will beat his drum. The next section 'Good Friday fare' rises to a drastic climax with the beach scene of fisherman, horse, eels, and sea-gulls, followed as it is by the death of Oskar's mother. From Oskar's point of view we have followed the relationship of his mother to the man she married, Alfred Matzerath from the Rhineland, and to her cousin Jan Bronski, who opted for Poland. Matzerath has 'the habit of always waving when others waved, of always shouting, laughing and clapping, when others shouted, laughed and clapped.' Bronski, whom Oskar would like to think of as his father, meets his death in the early phase of the war. The idyll of Oskar's childhood is now over. If Oskar's impassive literacy has an uncanny, intimidating effect, the people who are closest to him have warmth and sensibility, in spite of the distortions that the narrator's point of view cultivates. From 1939 onwards Oskar passes to a more adult, independent phase, which allows him to take part in a wartime entertainment group, to survive his father's death in 1945, to move to the West and to be suspected of responsibility for the death of the nurse Dorothea.

Katz und Maus (Cat and Mouse), 1961, is described by its author as a Novelle, no doubt an ironic harking back to an earlier tradition, like Oskar Matzerath's description of himself as a 'hero'. Formally this work has a concentrated narrative texture that is more disciplined than the exuberant heaping up of detail that characterizes parts of *Die Blechtrommel*. The Novelle has in Joachim Mahlke a central character who stands apart from his fellow schoolboys in the first place through his unusually large Adam's apple; from this feature stems his drive to distinguish himself, whether in adolescent sexuality, in swimming and exploring a sunk vessel, or in acquiring a war medal. Mahlke, seen from the point of view of his school companion Pilenz, remains a figure of mystery and sadness. His final disappearance leaves Pilenz with a long lasting sense of guilt and anxiety.

Hundejahre (Dog Years), 1963, is a novel of proportions comparable to those of *Die Blechtrommel*, and a work which covers a similar ground and time, from pre-war and war years in the Danzig area to the period of 1945 and after in West Germany. If the earlier novel depended on the narrative of Oskar Matzerath to give it unity of presentation, *Hundejahre* is more broadly based in its angles of vision, and consequently more colourful and varied in its material, though the exuberance and extravagance of the author's imagination may make it formally less concentrated. The novel falls into three sections, each with its separate focal points and narrative method. The boyhood friendship of Eddi Amsel and Walter Matern, both born in 1917, dominates the first section. Eddi Amsel's ability to make grotesque and impressive scarecrows thrives with the protection of Walter Matern, though the latter at times resents the secondary role he plays here. Even the starting of secondary school education at Danzig does not break the idyll; for there is the benign figure of the schoolmaster Oswald Brunies, who adopts the foundling infant Jenny Brunies at the close of this part. With the second section, the narrative switches to the point of view of Harry Liebenau as presented in a series of imagined love-letters to his cousin Tulla Pokriefke, his account beginning with the summer of 1932. Walter Matern, after a spell as a Communist supporter, becomes a National Socialist, while Eddi Amsel's partly Jewish background separates him from his erstwhile friend. Parallel to the beating-up of Amsel by Matern and his fellow-members of the S.A. is the maltreatment of Jenny Brunies by Tulla Pokriefke. Tulla, maladjusted since the death of her brother Konrad in the summer of 1933, is both promiscuous and dangerously malicious (it is she who is responsible for Brunies's imprisonment in a concentration camp). As the love-letters are replaced by a 'concluding fairy-tale', the second section becomes yet grimmer and more fantastic, until interest becomes directed primarily to the movements of the Führer's dog Prinz. Fantasy and political satire supervene in the final section of the novel, where Walter Matern's movements culminate in an intention to emigrate to East Germany, though a chance meeting with Eddi Amsel, now proprietor of a thriving subterranean scarecrow-factory, leads to a renewal of their long broken relationship. Grass has indeed fashioned a world of his own in these three prose works, which are linked together not only in their times and places, but also in some overlapping of characters. Incredible and repulsive in part, it is none the less a world which insistently lays claim to our attention.

With *Mutmaßungen über Jakob* (*Speculations about Jacob*), 1959, Uwe Johnson (born 1934) made an immediate impression by his treatment of the theme of divided Germany and by the stylistic and formal presentation of his material. Jakob Abs, a signalman at an important rail centre in East Germany, is killed as he goes across the lines on a foggy early morning in November, 1956. Certainty about his personality or about the reason for his death is not available. Authorial comment does not intervene to bring clarification from an omniscient distance, nor is the reader allowed direct insight into Jakob's own thoughts. Stretches, or snatches, of dialogue, narrative, and monologue involving people who knew Jakob offer 'speculations' about him. It is difficult reading, with unusual punctuation as a further barrier, yet with a compelling quality of poetry as it evokes a damp, everyday ordinariness of setting. Jakob and his mother came as refugees from further east in 1945 to a small coastal town on the Baltic, where they found a home, in what was to become part of the Democratic Republic, with Cresspahl and his daughter Gesine. Gesine goes to the West and works as an interpreter for NATO. Jakob's mother leaves the Democratic Republic too. But Jakob decides not to stay in the West; when Gesine says 'Stay here', he replies 'Come back with me.' She comments to Jonas, the university assistant: 'I would rather say: he for his part had become involved after the war with what we can call I suppose hope of a new beginning, he wanted to accept responsibility for it himself and also for the decision that was to be implied in that.' But not only Jacob is a subject of speculation; other characters, such as Gesine and the police-agent Rohlfs, have tantalizingly unexplained facets of thought and action.

Das dritte Buch über Achim (*The Third Book about Achim*), 1961, again centres upon difficulties of mutual understanding between East and West Germany, with a main figure whose personality is presented gradually and fragmentarily, so that the reader remains at the end without certainty that the interpretation offered to him is definite. Whereas Jakob in the *Mutmaßungen* is a character whose actions interest only a small circle, Achim is a public figure in the Democratic Republic, a star racing-cyclist and parliamentary representative. A journalist from Hamburg is to write a book on him (there have been two others already) which is to illustrate 'the collaboration of sport and of the power of society in one person.' The biographical data which the West German Karsch discovers to be salient features of Achim's past will clearly be unusable for the book he is supposed to be writing. As a boy he was a supporter of National Socialism, but had a friendship with a Jewish girl for a time. A Russian soldier makes him a present of a bicycle, but a three-speed gear for it is subsequently purchased illegally in West Berlin. On 20 July 1953, he became politically compromised in the Berlin uprising and received a prison sentence. Karsch as narrator builds upon the sparse clues he receives and tells the story of what he imagines happened on some of the occasions of Achim's life. It is not the outward fame of a popular figure that interests the narrator; instead it is the formation of a personality against a background of social and political change that is bewildering in its impact on the individual.

In a novel that is considerably less austere and complex than the two earlier ones, Johnson has responded to the challenge of the Berlin Wall in fictional form. *Zwei Ansichten* (*Two Views*), 1965, gives predominantly the points of view of a young man from the Federal Republic, a press-photographer, and of a young nurse from East Berlin. Their thoughts and feelings are fairly fully disclosed to the reader, so that these characters do not acquire the mysterious, and perhaps on that account awe-inspiring, even mythical qualities of Jakob Abs and Achim. Herr B. makes it possible for Fräulein D. to make an escape from East to West. The story has a conventional element, and yet there is an un-expected factor in that the feelings which the couple have for each other are, it seems, lukewarm and ambivalent. With the dry detail of his descriptions here, the author stands at a distance from any attempt at a simplified solution to the larger problems that are raised.

Peter Weiss (born 1916), dramatist and prose-writer, has given in two volumes a first-person account of an individual's develop-ment that is starkly written, full of the detail of daily life, and radical in its revolt against established order in social and private living. *Abschied von den Eltern* (English translation published as *Leave-taking*), 1961, opens with the protagonist making funeral arrangements for his businessman father, who has died in Ghent. The sense of alienation from his parents is immediately emphasized: 'In the life of this man there was an unceasing struggle to preserve home and family; amidst worries and illnesses he, together with his wife, clung to the possession of the home, without ever experiencing any happiness in this possession.' His mother, formerly an actress, is fearfully unpredictable in her moods, while his father is for the most part remote, bewildered by the reactions of a child who finds home and school a nightmare. The accidental death of his sister Margit, with whom the boy had an unusually close relationship, represents a family as well as a personal crisis, with which 'the journey into what was uncertain had begun.' It coincides with plans for emigration; his father, who is Jewish, sets up home and business first in England, then in Czechoslovakia, and finally in Sweden. For the narrator, being a refugee confirms the sense of not belonging that has long been with him. He begins to find fulfilment in painting and writing, feeling that the desire to be a revolutionary is being frustrated by the oppressive weight of 'old norms'. The narrative breaks off, however, with an expression of confidence that 'a transformation had taken place, that new forces were dominating my life'.

The novel *Fluchtpunkt* (*Vanishing Point*), 1962, continues the narrative of *Abschied von den Eltern*, confining itself for the most part to the years 1940–7 and being centred upon Stockholm. The protagonist struggles with his painting, at first with little success, though gradually he achieves some recognition. He wrestles with writing prose, and discusses some of the European authors whom he admires. He has periods as a farm-labourer and a lumberjack, commenting on the primitive conditions he finds in this rural environment. There is some work in connection with his father's business, but the short reunion of parents and son towards the end makes it clear that there is still little in common between the generations, although there is determination on both sides that old wounds shall not be re-opened. There are relations with women; his marriage with the daughter of a Swedish professional family eventually breaks up. His imagination is seeking precision of expression: 'Everything that happened to me was of such a nature that it could be recounted. There was nothing that lay outside the realm of the tangible. The greatest adventure was the construction of a clear, exact world.'

This volume too concludes with a mood of hope, when he goes to Paris and experiences the 'shock of freedom': 'On that evening early in 1947 on the embankment of the Seine in Paris at the age of thirty I saw that I could participate in an exchange of thoughts that was taking place round about, bound to no country.' More or less contemporary with these two volumes of narrative cast in the form of realistic autobiography are two shorter, self-contained prose works which are more in the nature of experimental studies. *Der Schatten des Körpers des Kutschers* ('The Shadow of the Coachman's Body'), 1960, allows a first-person narrator to record impressions observed in the course of a day spent in association with a small group of people. The emphasis is on close examination of physical states and processes which are presented with minimal reference to the emotional or cognitive factors that presumably accompany them. The reader is made aware of eating and drinking, of some aspects of physical labour and of ill-health, of a social evening with some unforeseen incidents, and of an act of copulation. *Das Gespräch der drei Gehenden* ('The Conversation of the Three Men Walking'), 1963, records the conversational exchanges, mostly consisting of incidents recalled from the past, of Abel, and Cabel, who are not brothers, but men who met by chance. Crossing a bridge evokes the memory of the ferryman who made a living before this bridge was built, and of the fortunes of his various sons. The work is a sequence of episodes, where not only the time-sequence but also the individual personality of the narrators are presented in fragmentary, blurred juxtaposition; the result is a wider extension of material, in place and time and viewpoint, than in *Der Schatten des Körpers des Kutschers*, though with a similar overall economy of presentation.

7 '... On behalf of this living together.' (Johannes Bobrowski)

ARNOLD ZWEIG (1887–1968) was the major novelist of the generation of Broch and Musil who chose East Germany as his home. He had left Germany in 1933, and was a refugee in various European countries, including Britain, and also in Palestine; he returned to live in East Berlin from 1948 onwards. *Das Beil von Wandsbek* (*The Axe of Wandsbek*), 1947, is the elaboration of a macabre incident reported from Hamburg in 1938. A suburban butcher consents to act as executioner to four political prisoners who are held in Fuhlsbüttel prison in order that he may save his business from bankruptcy by earning quick money. Its theme might have been more suitable for a satirical short story rather than for a novel. *Die Zeit ist reif* (*The Time Is Ripe*), 1957, is a mellow, broadly based work which gives an extended picture of life in Germany during the year immediately before the outbreak of war in 1914 and up to the early months of 1915. The central figures are the young lovers Werner Bertin and Lenore Wahl. They have met as students in Munich, and although they have much in common—literary, artistic, and intellectual interests, and a Jewish background—the differing situation of their two families leads to their relationship being kept secret from their parents. Werner Bertin, as son of a master joiner in Silesia, is socially unacceptable to Lenore's father, a wealthy Berlin business-man, though Bertin finds a good friend in her grandfather, Markus Wahl, who is percipient in business affairs and in the implications of political events. Bertin's gifts as a writer and thinker are appreciated by the old man who encourages him to write a 'treatise on God' to be entered as a prize-essay in Russia. This work, and also a stage-play of Bertin's, are prevented from gaining public recognition by the advent of the war. There is an idyllic quality about Bertin's life with Lenore, during their stay in South Tirol and Northern Italy in the summer of 1913 and their subsequent times together near Munich and in Berlin. Bertin's aesthetically based liberalism is seen as preventing him from obtaining the critical insight into contemporary political realities which some of his friends already have; during the winter of 1914–15 his way of life, and that of Lenore, can continue in Berlin as yet without being immediately threatened. The narrative also contains sections of commentary upon the international situation emanating from the informed sources of friends of the Wahls, the officers Clauß and Schieffenzahn. At the close of this work, the future of German-Austrian relations with Italy is in the balance. *Die Zeit ist reif* is designed as the first volume of the cycle constructed around *Der Streit um den Sergeanten Grischa* (English translation published as *The Case of Sergeant Grischa*), 1927, Zweig's novel of an episode from events on the Eastern front during the First World War, which made a major impact when it was first published. *Die Feuerpause* ('Interval between the Firing'), 1954, is a further volume in this sequence. Werner Bertin and his companions are spending November and December 1917 in a state of inactive suspense on the Eastern front, as preparations are made for the peace-talks at Brest-Litovsk between Germany and the representatives of the new Russian government. There is at first the hope that the negotiations may lead to a general European settlement, but by the end of the year this expectation has become remote. Much of the novel is taken up with social gatherings of the small group of friends where Werner Bertin recounts incidents from his experiences in Serbia and then on the Western front. These flash-backs to an earlier stage of the war usually illustrate aspects of intolerance and prejudice in the administration of ordinary soldiers' lives. *Die Feuerpause* suffers somewhat from the discursive way in which its material is assembled, and lacks the freshness and variety of the author's portrayal of the end of the pre-war era in *Die Zeit ist reif*.

Johannes R. Becher (born 1891), an active supporter of proletarian revolution throughout the time of the Weimar Republic, became a leading literary figure in the Democratic Republic. His reputation has been firstly as a lyrical poet. His novel *Abschied* ('Parting'), 1940, subtitled 'a German tragedy: 1900–1914', is somewhat loosely constructed, and remains in the memory as a succession of episodes rather than as a closely knit whole. As a small boy Hans is allowed to stay up to welcome the new year and the new, twentieth, century. 'Things must be different'; his grandmother's words are a toast to the new age. But the boy can see no changes at breakfast next morning, and life in this conventional, prosperous home, dominated by an unimaginative, ambitious, and irritable father, is strait-laced within narrow, intolerant circumstances. The boy's lively intelligence, combined with an emotionally rooted antagonism to his father's personality, develops into a distrust of the social background with which his father identifies himself. Hans himself is shown as unfavourably influenced in part by this environment, as in his betrayal of the poorer boy Hartinger, who had been his friend at the primary school. In adolescence his perplexity and distrust of the values current in society around him bring him into a despairing defiance, before he finds his life's purpose in embracing the cause of revolutionary socialism. His rejection of the attitude of most of his countrymen to the outbreak of war in 1914 is more decided than the more gradual and more differentiated disillusionment which befalls Zweig's hero Werner Bertin.

East German authors who can look back to the era before 1914 may be expected to portray the changes in society from the early years of the present century onwards in colours which would contrast the inadequacies of earlier forms of German society, culminating in National Socialism, with the new hope they find in the Democratic Republic. Willi Bredel (1902–64) is the author of a trilogy *Verwandte und Bekannte* ('Relations and Acquaintances'), 1943–53, which narrates the fortunes of factory and dock workers in Hamburg in the years before 1914 and the struggles of the next generation to spread their Russophile beliefs during the Weimar Republic, while the third volume follows the adventures of Communist resisters to National Socialism. Bodo Uhse (1904–63) published a semi-autobiographical novel of an adolescence during the First World War, *Wir Söhne* (1947), written with freshness of style and feeling. *Die Patrioten* (1954) deals with the German–Russian conflict from the point of view of German underground opposition to Hitler.

Anna Seghers (born 1900) has been well known for a long time as an exponent of the proletarian novel, her most popular work being probably the war-time *Das siebte Kreuz* ('The Seventh Cross'), 1942. After emigrating to France, and then to Mexico, she returned to live in East Germany after the war. *Transit* (1944) deals with the plight of German refugees desperately seeking means of escape from Marseilles in 1940–1. *Die Toten bleiben jung* (*The Dead Stay Young*), 1949, takes a broad canvas and depicts a multiplicity of events and personages. Opening with the revolutionary movement in Berlin 1918 and concluding with the entry of the Russians there in 1945, this work reflects the principal political and social tendencies through the private lives of the contrasting groups of characters, working-class, peasantry, and industrialist and military bourgeoisie. A woman who loses her husband in 1918 and whose only son is killed in action in the Russian campaign of the Second World War remains faithful to their Communist cause and is rewarded by the arrival of the Russians in Berlin in 1945. The novel achieves a dramatic climax of some power in the final sections describing the Russian advance westwards. This is a professional and competent piece of writing, comparable to *War and Peace* in its structure, and showing Hitler's invasion of Russia as a repetition of Napoleon's campaign of 1812, though, almost inevitably, falling short of Tolstoy's masterpiece in humanity and wisdom.

Der Ausflug der toten Mädchen ('The Outing of the Dead Girls'), 1948, is the title of a volume in which Anna Seghers depicts, in black and white terms, the suffering of political resisters to the Nazi régime. The story which provides the title looks back to a school outing, and links the memory of friends as they were in their youth with their subsequent fates. Another convincing tale is 'Die Saboteure', which tells of the life of workers in a munitions factory in Mainz during the war. Anna Seghers's three tales, *Die Linie* (1950), published with a birthday greeting to Stalin, are political propaganda rather than literature; the little collection of *Friedensgeschichten* ('Peace Stories'), 1950, are interesting for their reflection of life in East Germany at that period. These and others of Anna Seghers's shorter tales were collected under the title *Der Bienenstock* ('The Beehive'), 1953.

Die Entscheidung ('The Decision'), 1959, retains some characters from *Die Toten bleiben jung*, and is a *Zeitroman* that is comparable in its structure. Its central theme is the re-opening and gradual development of a factory's production during the early years of the Democratic Republic up to 1951. Parallel with this narrative is the account of the Bentheim works under capitalist management in the Federal Republic. In the West difficulties arise chiefly in relationships between management and factory-workers. The factory at Kossin, in East Germany, has its problems too, though the author is at pains to demonstrate the emergence of a group loyalty that will overcome adverse material conditions. The major crisis in this part of the action arises when intrigue brings about the defection of a group of engineers to the West, though prompt governmental intervention and the co-operation of the workers are shown as succeeding in making good this loss. Three of the characters have associations going back to shared experiences in the Spanish Civil War. Richard Hagen, now a senior official, appears in the opening section to inaugurate the rehabilitation of the Kossin factory and again towards the close in order to help in the crisis. Robert Lohse's fortunes, as a worker in the factory, are followed more closely, and the problems of his personal relations have considerable prominence. Their former comrade Herbert Melzer has chosen to live in the West, as a writer and reporter of some popularity with American readers; however, a return to Europe arouses in him a renewal of left-wing sympathies which alienates him from his Western associates and leads to his death after participating in a Bentheim strike demonstration. A further strand of narrative traces the tensions between Riedl, an engineer who remains faithful to the East, and his wife

Katharina who is in the West. The development of various young people is watched: the orphan Thomas, the Mexican boy Miguel, Herbert Melzer's nephew Jochen Schneider, and his niece Liesel. The action of the novel is spread over many characters, and the multiplicity of plots and places makes the links between some of the incidents rather tenuous. As an epic of the early years of the Democratic Republic *Die Entscheidung* probably has in the first place historical interest.

With *Nackt unter Wölfen* (*Naked Among Wolves*), 1958, Bruno Apitz (born 1900) has constructed a strongly dispassionate novel of life in a concentration camp during the last few weeks before the end of the war. A detailed description of life in a strange and grim community is given, with a mounting pressure of tension among guards and prisoners as the American forces approach more closely. The hierarchy of the SS-guards, with their various specialities and their mistrust of one another, their intrigues to maintain or extend their own policies and influence, and their differing reactions to an awareness that their present way of life will shortly be abruptly halted and the captors of today will be the wanted men of tomorrow, forms one unit, complex enough, but increasingly aware that, if the thousands of prisoners are in many ways their helpless victims, their presence and the activities of a few captives can be a real threat to them. The Communist resistance group among the prisoners appears as the centre of active opposition to the guards, showing skill and individual enterprise in the collecting of information and in the preservation of their organization. With their secret stores of weapons they are awaiting a suitable moment for undertaking the overthrowal of their oppressors; if they revolt too soon, or too late, they may be exposing themselves and their fellow-prisoners to mass annihilation. Their leader Bochow says: '"Those human beings who leave the barbed wire of the concentration camps behind them alive will be the advance troops of a juster world. We don't know what is coming. No matter what the world will look like afterwards, it will be a juster one, or else we must despair of the reason of mankind."' The hazardous situation is further complicated by the arrival of a small child, brought in a suitcase by a prisoner who has been evacuated from Auschwitz. In spite of Bochow's misgivings, the group decide to look after the boy and conceal his presence from the guards. The issue becomes a major challenge to the initiative of those who accept responsibility for protecting the child, and to the guards themselves, once their suspicions about the situation have been aroused. The narrative portrays a society of inmates and captors which is labyrinthine and mobile, but where a semblance of 'normality', of the maintenance of a régime of 'order', is eerily asserted even when it is known that its destruction must come in the very near future. The mood of the narrative is unsensational, even dry, but controlled and purposeful; the situations are seen with vivid detail as well as with an awareness of their relevance to a complex whole.

Authors of the older generation who could, if they wished, take themes embodying Communist working-class reactions to events before 1945 were in a position to provide models for prose writing after the establishment of the Democratic Republic. In their experiences during emigration they would have much in common with novelists such as Thomas and Heinrich Mann. Their use of the *Zeitroman* in a spirit of documentary realism was evidently close to the approach of H. W. Richter and of the mood of the 'Gruppe 47' in its early phase. Hans Peter Anderle[1] has referred to this as the first of three trends discernible in East German writing in the twenty years following 1945, with the *caveat* (which the present writer can but underline) that 'even for the person of good will the development of contemporary literature, being in an incessant flux, is only comprehensible in a limited way'. The socialist realism of these writers aligns the documentary, descriptive approach with materialism and determinism combined with a forward-looking hopefulness about the realization of the good society through unqualified co-operation with the state's directives. With the 'thaw' of 1956–7 came the desire to broaden the scope of literature, and the 'Bitterfeld

1 Hans Peter Anderle, *Mitteldeutsche Erzähler. Eine Studie mit Proben und Porträts*. Cologne, 1965, cf. pp. 9–26.

movement' arising out of a conference held in 1959, and re-affirmed five years later, aimed to associate professional writers more closely with industrial and other economic problems of the country, while encouraging the workers engaged in production to take more interest in literature, particularly in the context of its being harnessed to contemporary living. A third phase might be seen in the hesitant emergence of a preoccupation with the hitherto disregarded concerns of the individual of artistic, intro-spective or satirical personality.

Bertolt Brecht (1898–1956) returned in 1948 to East Germany after his exile. In his prose collection of *Kalendergeschichten* (*Tales from the Calendar*), 1949, he reflected moods and backgrounds comparable to those of his great dramas. The dry wit of the aphorisms of the 'Stories of Herr Keuner' has been widely appreciated. The tales and verse of this volume, told with a deliberately bare simplicity that is by no means naïve artlessness, consciously hark back to the instructive tone of the early nine-teenth-century *Kalender*, or almanacs, which aimed at reaching the widest public. The novel fragment *Die Geschäfte des Herrn Julius Caesar* ('The Business Affairs of Mr. Julius Caesar'), 1957, which was written in Denmark in 1938 and 1939 and published posthumously, is rather less likely to have a wide appeal. Twenty years after the death of Julius Caesar a young man who is engaged on writing his biography pays a visit to Mummlius Spicer, formerly bailiff and later banker, to one of Caesar's old legionaries and to a poet who also has memories of the man who has become a quasi-legendary figure. The monumental approach which would like to see Caesar as a great man has to be on the defensive against the scepticism of those who knew him. For Spicer Caesar was a man who was always in need of money, and Roman history is seen to have been predominantly influenced by commercial interests and monetary speculations. The inset narrative within this framework consists of diaries written by Caesar's secretary Rarus, which Spicer allows the narrator to read; Julius Caesar's manoeuvres at the time of the Catiline conspiracy, his relationship with Pompey and other contemporaries, and his year in Spain are interpreted in terms of financial and political in-fighting. Although the narrative method does not allow us to come close to the man, he is evidently a Brechtian figure, with some resemblances to Pierpont Mauler in the play *Die heilige Johanna der Schlachthöfe* or to the central figure of *Leben des Galilei*. The element of parody and irony combined with the evocation of an exotic historical setting is familiar to readers of Brecht, but provides an atmosphere that is quite different from that of Anna Seghers's work.

Realistic treatment of themes from country life is a particular characteristic of some of the work of Erwin Strittmatter (born 1912, in Spremberg, Niederlausitz). His *Ochsenkutscher* ('Ox-Ploughman'), 1950, is comparable to Graf's *Unruhe um einen Friedfertigen* in its evocation of day-to-day life, including the impact of political events, upon a rural community, for the most part during the Weimar Republic. Strittmatter's male characters have as an alternative to working as labourers on Herr von Rendsburg's estate the possibility of employment in the nearby coalmine; but their living conditions are in either case depressed, and these villagers are unable to express themselves with the independence of Graf's Bavarian country people. *Ochsenkutscher* consists of a series of episodes, largely centring upon the boyhood and youth of Lope and the way he is moulded by varying influences. In rejecting the traditionalist outlook represented by the estate landlord, he is also putting himself at a distance from Liepe, his nominal father, and associating himself with the scepticism of his mother and with the left-wing commitment of his uncle Blemska. As 1933 approaches, National Socialism plays an increasing part in local affairs, while von Rendsburg and his family, though standing apart from the newer movement, are shown as losing their earlier dominant influence over the neighbourhood. The narrative manner is direct and abrupt, with frequent use of dialogue. *Ole Bienkopp* (1963) takes as its material a village community in Eastern Germany during the years after 1945. A large cast of characters is deployed with ingenuity and vigour, and farming problems and personal relations are often set in the context of political issues. Ole Hansen, born in 1905, acquired the nickname 'Bienkopp' on account of his youthful, obstinate enthusiasm for bee-keeping. In middle life, as a respected and public-spirited farmer, he suffers from the follies of his wife Anngret and of her lover Ramsch, who is suspected of having been responsible for the apparently accidental death of the local Party secretary, Anton Dürr. The first half of the novel concludes with the disappearance of Ramsch to the West, and with Ole being officially reproved for introducing a form of collective farming into the locality on his own initiative. Part Two sees the community happily rid of the undesirable Ramsch, but the malice and pettiness of some Party officials becomes an obstacle to Ole's well-being, even after his collective-farming venture has been publicly praised after the general Party policy has changed. Ole's late happiness in love with Märthe Mattusch is terminated by his death after a final exhausting effort of self-imposed labour. Many of the episodes are narrated in a tone of boisterous humour, though with idyllic approaches on occasions. With the death of Anton Dürr at the beginning the mantle of responsible leadership in the community, identified with the spirit rather than the letter of Party law, passes to Ole, who struggles to shoulder it until his own end.

Dieter Noll (born 1927) has presented in *Die Abenteuer des Werner Holt* ('The Adventures of Werner Holt'), 1964, an account of a young man's personal development against the background of the later war years and the early post-war period. The first volume, following the hero's experiences from schooldays in May 1943 through his involvement with the war until the capitulation of two years later, forms a unit dominated by a sequence of vivid episodes. After a time as anti-aircraft assistant near Essen, Holt is transferred to Czechoslovakia, then attached to a tank-corps, and is to be caught up in a series of hectic adventures as the Russians advance from the east. There is effective acceleration and intensification as the action rises to its final climax. The second volume, a 'novel of a return home', shows Holt's uncertain seeking for purpose and stability in his life. His first attempt to rehabilitate himself under the guidance of his father and of the latter's colleagues at an East German pharmaceutical factory fails. Holt makes a fresh start near Hamburg, where his mother, who has for some time been divorced from his father, can provide him with contacts with influential business circles. After adventures in West Germany, Holt returns to the Democratic Republic, where he decides to remain. The war-time adventures are given shape by Holt's continuing association with schoolfriends, in particular with Gomulka, who makes his way to the Russians, with Vetter, who in the second volume becomes fatefully caught up in criminal activities, and with Wolzow, whose militarist enthusiasm has a magnetic effect upon many whom he encounters. Holt's early, unthinking adherence to the German war-time outlook is gradually dispelled, and his re-education towards the acceptance of Communism is the main theme of the second volume. If Wolzow's relationship with Holt had been one of ambivalence, in the sequel Holt finds himself again in a comparable position with regard to Schneidereit, a confident representative of the official viewpoint who is also Holt's rival in love. Holt is still largely an individualist when the novel closes, though presumably, if with some uncertainty, on the way towards settling down in his personal life and in his attitude to the outlook of the state.

Der geteilte Himmel ('The Divided Heaven' [Sky]), 1963, by Christa Wolf (born 1929) gives the impression of being a conscious reply to Uwe Johnson's *Mutmaßungen über Jakob*. Johnson's Jakob went to West Germany to join the young woman who was already established there, then came back and died shortly afterwards in mysterious circumstances. Christa Wolf's heroine Rita visits Manfred Herrfurth, a chemical engineer who has recently gone to West Berlin and invited her to join him there; she returns to East Germany, where she collapses from the emotional strain, but later recovers and readjusts herself to a positive attitude to living, without Manfred, in the Democratic Republic. The crucial action takes place during 1961; the erection of the Berlin Wall is, however, only incidental, for Rita's decisions are not affected by this outside event. She has already had earlier misgivings about the complete compatibility of her relationship with Manfred. His academic acquaintances and his family background, not to speak of his own scepticism, are less sympathetic to her, for she spontaneously accepts the community of the workers' brigade at the factory and the guidance of her tutor at the teachers' training college. If imperfections in the day-to-day efficiency of this society are recognized, the long-term objectives receive her full support. However, Rita's moods are privately and emotionally orientated, and expressed with strongly subjective intensity.

Johannes Bobrowski (1917–65) was one of the few authors of his generation whose work was received with equal warmth in both East and West Germany. After the end of the war he was in Russian captivity until 1950, when he settled in East Berlin, as publisher's reader to the Union-Verlag. He first became widely known as a lyrical poet, declaring Klopstock to be his principal model, with his major commitment in theme being the wish to bring greater understanding of the problems involved in the relations between Germans and their eastern neighbours. *Levins Mühle* (*Levin's Mill*), 1964, is his major prose work, a novel of considerable originality and insight, which is set in a rural area not far from the German–Russian frontier of its time, 1874. The grandfather, a prosperous German miller, ruthlessly puts his young competitor, Levin, out of business, but this challenges Habedank, a nomadic violin-player who is father of Levin's beloved, Marie, to incite Poles and other sympathizers to protest against the offender. The focal points of the action are three group occasions—a christening celebration, a circus entertainment, and a church festivity, where the fairly large cast of the novel's characters can be brought together and effectively deployed. Although both Levin and the grandfather finally leave the district, the community still remains united, in spite of the tensions between the two opposing groups. The work is written with a style combining the lyrical evocation of nature, in particular of the birds, and of human emotion, with a darting humour. Interpolated in the main narrative are a series of visionary 'hauntings' that befall the grandfather on occasions when he is unconscious and recall episodes involving his ancestors in earlier centuries, while the twentieth-century grandson who tells the story provides a present-day perspective. The whole is filled with vitality and gracefulness, to which the narrator, making full use of traditional omniscience and giving his account in the present tense, adds his effective contribution, not least by the narrative landmarks of the '34 sentences about my grandfather.' The posthumously published novel *Litauische Claviere* ('Lithuanian Pianos'), 1966, is set in Memel in 1936, and reflects Bobrowski's interest in the history and folklore of his childhood environment. The musician Gawehn and the schoolmaster Voigt are planning to collaborate on an opera with an eighteenth-century Lithuanian subject, but this is a time when relationships between the nationalities are sorely tried by the disrupting impact of Nazi activities. As Gawehn muses:

So many good people and so much effort: on behalf of this living-together. So much worry, but so much good will as well,—what has it brought in finally?

And is it this particular day that is meant by finally?

8 CONCLUSION

WITH the end of the war in 1945 and the occupation of Germany by the Allied authorities it seemed as if there might be little or no room for the fruitful furtherance of creative writing in German, whether in the novel or in other genres. Conditions in daily life were such that literary publication was bound to be fraught with unusual difficulties, and that in these circumstances the possibilities of an extended novel being made available to readers would be remoter than the likelihood of presentation which a volume of verse might expect. If the voices of refugee authors were now heard again, it might seem that the return of their different emphasis, pointing to traditions from the time of the Weimar Republic, would be more of a shock than a positive stimulus for those who had remained in Central Europe from 1933 onwards. The confrontation between these two groups—those who had left and those who had stayed—seemed to point to a formidable barrier, which stressed sharp divisions in attitudes and experiences. Thomas Mann, for instance, remained until his death in 1955 unwilling to enter into any kind of informal communication with literary figures who were not fairly closely associated with his own point of view, although he had done much to support and encourage many writers who had become refugees like himself. At that time too writers associated with the term 'inner emigration' would pay little attention to those of their generation who had left Germany in the 1930s. Their styles and themes differed. Bergengruen, Ernst Jünger, Le Fort, and Wiechert wrote in a traditional style, elevated and complex at times, and often separated from the everyday idiom; they could continue to write as they had written before 1945, and could now find a wider and more direct appraisal of their work than had been possible earlier. But as time went on, readers would miss as direct an approach to contemporary realism in these writers as that presented by some younger authors. If Bergengruen or Le Fort preferred traditionally narrated historical novels and tales, it was partly because this mode of writing was sympathetic to them and has permitted them a certain amount of political criticism during the 1930s, and partly because historical fiction has had a considerable appeal to their readers.

For the younger man who wanted to take up writing the period immediately after 1945 presented particular difficulties. The reading public might well feel a first need to become orientated in both the national and the international literary scene. After twelve years of restrictive censorship, people would wish to make acquaintance with authors who wrote in German and who had been virtually inaccessible until after 1945; Kafka had become a figure of international significance, but the texts of his writings were still to be explored. Beyond the German language itself, the rediscovery of international trends and authors was pursued with considerable eagerness, encouraged by the 're-education' programmes of American, British, and French occupation authorities; in East Germany, with a predominantly Marxist emphasis, Russian literary tradition would be appreciated. There might seem to be little enough opportunity, in these circumstances, for the younger generation to obtain a hearing. On the other hand the opportunity was there, and also the inner need to put into imaginative writing a distillation of the great pressure of experiences that had been forced upon people in Central Europe by National Socialism, the war and its aftermath. The preoccupations of the older generation, whether of the 'outer' or 'inner' emigration, were also theirs, to some extent, especially the haunting concern for the events of the recent past and a sense of responsibility for what had been during the Nazi period. However, the then younger generation wished to speak directly of their experiences, and what was then new material, the particular contemporary reality known to them at first hand, had not been as yet been given imaginative shape. A number of authors of the 'Gruppe 47' began in this way, but they were not the only ones. For them there was to be the 'Kahlschlag', the cutting down and clearing away of the existing trees, so that a new start could be made, as Hans Werner Richter termed it. With 'zero-point' behind them the realism of the late 1940s would be concerned to purify language of artifice or of usages associated with National Socialism, and to look dispassionately, though with a spirit of humane sympathy, at the life they knew around them. Political comment was again possible, and the *Zeitroman* could contain this; a central character or group of characters could be followed in their development from childhood to early middle age, against the impact of various public events of the 1930s and 1940s. After the war would come the return home, with the need for re-adjustment to what appeared to be a radically changed environment and possibly for a transformation of personal outlook on life. The man coming back home would feel estranged from the life going on around him; he might eventually become reconciled to it, or he might remain critically apart, suspicious of any suggestion that he should become re-integrated with this world. Such a reaction, spontaneous in the circumstances, would be an alignment of a new generation of writers into a long tradition of the artists' mistrust of the social framework into which most of their contemporaries fitted; the reactions of Goethe's Werther and Rilke's Malte found their successors here. With National Socialism there had been a totalitarian structure of society that was subsequently wholly discredited. Was it not likely that a novelist would regard the system that replaced it with some misgivings too? Or that any social system at all would be looked at askance?

The rebuilding of West Germany after the establishment of the Federal Republic took place without much direct encouragement from younger authors. Looking back from the mid-1960s, Böll could see the interim period of 1945–8 as a time of promise and potentiality. The nightmare repressiveness of Nazism had gone, and the direction which any new German form of government might take was not yet established. In this interlude, grim as it was in many respects, there yet lay the seed of an unknown future, one that was less predictable than in many other European countries, and one in which an ideal of sympathy and tolerant understanding might be realized. Schaper has referred to the years 1949–51 as a time when the German reading public was welcoming and ready to go in search of its authors. However, the pattern of life in the 1950s, the first decade of the 'economic miracle', saw many novelists reaffirming their feeling of separation from a society which they saw as being rebuilt with a view to the restoration of old traditions that were better abandoned and to the eager absorption of technological developments of a world-wide character. The realism might contain evident appeals for the reader's support of the author's social commitment expressed in terms of direct emotionalism. Or the element of fantasy might supervene, with lightness and gentleness sometimes, or with harsh grotesqueness at other times. Both realism and fantasy could move into the realm of satire, and as the 1950s drew to a close, a darker mood, a fiercer realism, and a more bitter form of mockery came to the fore, often presented with a high degree of professional skill. These trends have not been confined to Germany, of course, nor have they necessarily been exaggerated there; but they have been constituent factors in the work of a number of novelists.

The satirical sharpness and disillusionment in the writing of Koeppen and Arno Schmidt in the early 1950s anticipated the massivity of attack in Grass's *Die Blechtrommel* of 1959. The 'coming to terms with the past' of National Socialism was expressed in this *Zeitroman* in conjunction with a ferocity of realistic accumulation, and with a use of the grotesque and fantastic, that was likely to be overwhelming. Oskar Matzerath was a half-hero, or anti-hero, who seemed to represent the artist-outsider in hitherto unprecedented terms. The year 1959 also saw the publication of Martin Walser's extended and disillusioned portrayal of a contemporary business milieu, *Halbzeit*, as well as Böll's summary of three generations of a professional family's life, *Billard um halbzehn*. In that year too appeared Johnson's *Mutmaßungen über Jakob*, a reckoning with the problems of the division of Germany presented with distancing narrative methods. It might be permissible to see in these and other works of that time a culmination of trends in the German novel from 1945 onwards, an achievement of skilful and sustained formal presentation using thematic material and indicating attitudes that belonged essentially to that time and place. If the traditional realistic panorama viewing many facets of society was favoured by East German authors such as Anna Seghers and Arnold Zweig, the novel in the West was open to experiments which would reveal as problematic the individual's sense of identity and time.

In the 1960s came a new approach to drama in Germany which emphasized the factual and documentary in the context of topical political and social issues. Novels, however, had been a vehicle for such content from 1945 onwards. There could be the deliberate concentration on the sense-impressions of everyday life, on the revelation of ordinary things to the apparent exclusion of speculation, psychological analysis or imagination. If Peter Weiss's two autobiographical novels are too personal as documents to be seen under this rubric, his *Der Schatten des Körpers des Kutschers* seems to go far towards the elimination of thought and feeling in favour of sense-data. But fantasy can still be very much interwoven into the pattern of Grass's *Hundejahre* or Frisch's *Mein Name sei Gantenbein*.

Story-telling of a traditional kind has of course continued during these twenty years, and a fanciful experiment does not necessarily impress the reader more than a well told tale. Gaiser has recalled that: '... in spite of the much heralded "crisis" of the novel, in spite of the widespread doubts whether story-telling is of any significance, ... the reader can still derive naïve pleasure from feeling empathy, from following the course of events, from being diverted. If narrative art is experiencing a crisis, then certainly it is not one of the reader's making.'[1] Siegfried Lenz, for instance, has moved through the 1950s and 1960s with careful craftsmanship, and without being over-impressed by the extravagant. Gaiser, in the same essay, defends the positive qualities of

1 Gerd Gaiser, 'The Present Quandary of German Novelists', in: Robert R. Heitner (ed.), *The Contemporary Novel in German. A Symposium*, p. 68.

human nature against the predominance of malice and unpleasant-ness that he finds in much contemporary literature, pointing out that 'experience teaches that less real effort is expended while one is wielding the pen in anger than while guiding it along in a calm frame of mind'. German writers since 1945 have had to make more abrupt and radical adjustments to circumstances and ideas of concern to them than authors in some other countries. The challenge of the recent past seemed to be imperative in its demand for a response, and it was a situation that did not have a precise parallel in other literatures at that time. In due course the im-mediacy of this particular challenge became less demanding, and took its place along with other concerns and reactions that were frequently international, having their parallels elsewhere in the world too. Certainly the twenty years' novel writing, or rather, that portion of it that has been the main concern of this essay, has shown variety and vigour, breadth and concentrated poetic quality, realism and fantasy. One might hazard the guess that the German novel can rarely have gone through a period of more outstanding creative energy than it has done in the two decades following 1945.

SELECT BIBLIOGRAPHY

Abbreviations used for periodicals:

BA	=	*Books Abroad*
DU	=	*Der Deutschunterricht*
DVjs	=	*Deutsche Vierteljahresschrift für Literaturwissenschaft und Geistesgeschichte*
EG	=	*Etudes Germaniques*
FMLS	=	*Forum for Modern Language Studies*
GLL	=	*German Life and Letters, New Series*
GQ	=	*German Quarterly*
GR	=	*Germanic Review*
ML	=	*Modern Languages*
MLN	=	*Modern Language Notes*
MLQ	=	*Modern Language Quarterly*
MLR	=	*Modern Language Review*
PMLA	=	*Publications of the Modern Language Society of America*
WW	=	*Wirkendes Wort*
ZDP	=	*Zeitschrift für Deutsche Philologie*

GENERAL (Place of publication London unless otherwise stated)

Abbé, Derek Maurice Van, *Image of a People*, 1964.

Anderle, Hans Peter, *Mitteldeutsche Erzähler. Eine Studie mit Proben und Porträts.* Cologne, 1965.

Bance, A. F., 'The German Novel since 1945 and the Concept of Realism'. Dissertation Cambridge, 1968.

Bateman, J. A., 'The West German Novel, 1945–55, in its Presentation of Contemporary Conditions'. Dissertation Exeter, 1969.

Bettex, Albert, *Die Literatur der deutschen Schweiz von heute.* Zürich, 1950.

Bienek, Horst (ed.), *Werkstattgespräche mit Schriftstellern.* Munich, 1962.

Bithell, Jethro, *Modern German Literature 1880–1950.* 3rd ed., 1959.

Boeschenstein, H., *The German Novel, 1939–1944.* Toronto, 1949.

—— *Der neue Mensch. Die Biographie im deutschen Nachkriegsroman.* Heidelberg, 1958.

—— 'Contemporary German-Swiss Fiction'. GLL, vol. 12, 1958–59, pp. 24–33.

Closs, August (ed.), *Twentieth Century German Literature* (vol. 4 of *Introduction to German Literature*, general editor, August Closs), 1969.

Friederich, Werner P., *An Outline-History of German Literature.* 2nd ed., New York, 1961.

Grenzmann, Wilhelm, *Deutsche Dichtung der Gegenwart.* Frankfurt, 1953.

—— *Dichtung und Glaube.* 2nd ed., Bonn, 1952.

Hamburger, Michael, *From Prophecy to Exorcism. The Premisses of Modern German Literature,* 1965.

Hatfield, Henry, *Crisis and Continuity in Modern German Fiction.* Ithaca and London, 1969.

Heitner, Robert R. (ed.), *The Contemporary Novel in German. A Symposium.* Austin and London, Texas, 1967.

Holthusen, Hans Egon, *Der unbehauste Mensch. Motive und Probleme der modernen Literatur.* Munich, 1951.

Horst, K. A., *Die deutsche Literatur der Gegenwart.* Munich, 1957.

Jens, Walter, *Deutsche Literatur der Gegenwart.* Munich, 1961.

Keith-Smith, Brian (ed.), *Essays on Contemporary German Literature.* 1966.

Kieser, Rolf, 'Gegenwartsliteratur der deutschen Schweiz'. GQ, vol. 41, 1968, pp. 71–83.

Kindermann, Heinz (ed.), *Wegweiser durch die moderne Literatur in Österreich.* Innsbruck, 1954.

Klieneberger, H. R., *The Christian Writers of the Inner Emigration.* The Hague and Paris, 1968.

Klotz, Volker (ed.), *Zur Poetik des Romans.* Darmstadt, 1965.

Kunisch, Hermann (ed.), *Handbuch der deutschen Gegenwartsliteratur.* Munich, 1965.

Kutzbach, Karl August (ed.), *Autorenlexikon der Gegenwart.* Bonn, 1950.

Lange, Victor, *Modern German Literature 1870–1940.* Ithaca, New York, 1945.

Lennartz, Franz, *Deutsche Dichter und Schriftsteller der Zeit.* 10th ed., Stuttgart, 1969.

Livingstone, Rodney, 'German Literature from 1945'. In: *Periods in German Literature,* ed. J. M. Ritchie, 1966, pp. 283–305.

Majut, Rudolf, 'Geschichte des deutschen Romans vom Biedermeier bis zur Gegenwart'. In: *Deutsche Philologie im Aufriß*. Berlin, Bielefeld and Munich, vol. 2, 1954.

Martin, Jacques, 'Romans et romanciers de l'Allemagne d'après-guerre'. *Etudes Germaniques*, vol. 8, 1953, pp. 141–65.

Martini, Fritz, *Deutsche Literaturgeschichte von den Anfängen bis zur Gegenwart*. 15th ed., Stuttgart, 1968.

—— 'Der gegenwärtige Roman und das Problem der Tradition'. DU, vol. 14, no. 1, 1962, pp. 5–23.

Mönnig, Richard (ed.), *Translations from the German. English 1948–1964*. 2nd ed., Göttingen, 1968.

Muschg, Walter, *Die Zerstörung der deutschen Literatur*. Berne, 1956.

Osterle, Heinz D., 'The Other Germany: Resistance to the Third Reich in German Literature'. GQ, vol. 41, 1968, pp. 1–22.

Pascal, Roy, *The German Novel*. Manchester, 1956.

Reich-Ranicki, Marcel, *Deutsche Literatur in West und Ost*. Munich, 1963.

Schoolfield, George C., 'Exercises in Brotherhood: The Recent Austrian Novel'. GQ, vol. 26, 1953, pp. 228–40.

Soergel, Albert and Hohoff, Curt, *Dichtung und Dichter der Zeit*. Vol. 2, Düsseldorf, 1963.

Thomas, R. Hinton and Van Der Will, W., *The German Novel and the Affluent Society*. Manchester, 1968.

Welzig, Werner, *Der deutsche Roman im 20. Jahrhundert*. Stuttgart, 1967.

Winslow, J. D., 'The Depiction of the National Socialist State in the Post-War German Novel'. Dissertation Birmingham, 1964.

Winter, Helmut, 'East German Literature'. In: *Essays on Contemporary German Literature*, ed. Brian Keith-Smith, 1966, pp. 261–80.

Zimmermann, Werner, *Deutsche Prosadichtung der Gegenwart. Interpretationen für Lehrende und Lernende*. Düsseldorf, 1954–6.

Ziolkowski, Theodore, *Dimensions of the Modern Novel. German Texts and European Contexts*. Princeton, 1969.

STUDIES OF INDIVIDUAL WRITERS

AICHINGER, ILSE:
Alldridge, J. C., *Ilse Aichinger*, 1969.
Bedwell, Carol B., 'Who is the Bound Man? Towards an Interpreta-

tion of Ilse Aichinger's "Der Gefesselte".' GQ, vol. 38, 1965, pp. 30–7.

ANDERSCH, ALFRED:

Hesse, Walter G., Introduction to edition of Andersch, *Sansibar oder der letzte Grund*, 1964.

Weber, Werner, *Über Alfred Andersch*. Zürich, 1968.

ANDRES, STEFAN:

Hennecke, Hans, and others, *Stefan Andres. Eine Einführung in sein Werk*. Munich, 1962.

BECHER, JOHANNES:

Andrews, R. C., 'A Novel from Eastern Germany'. GLL, vol. 5, 1951–2, pp. 286–91.

BENN, GOTTFRIED:

Ashton, E. B. (ed.), *Primal Vision. Selected Writings of Gottfried Benn*. Norfolk, Connecticut, n.d.

Hamburger, Michael, 'Gottfried Benn'. In: *Reason and Energy*, 1957, pp. 275–312.

Hilton, Ian, 'Gottfried Benn'. In: *German Men of Letters*, vol. 3, ed. Alex Natan, 1964, pp. 129–50.

BERGENGRUEN, WERNER:

Alexander, M., 'Werner Bergengruen: Artistry and Theme'. Dissertation Oxford, 1966.

Brown, M. W. F., 'Werner Bergengruen'. ML, vol. 37, 1955–6, pp. 11–14.

Hofacker, Erich, 'Justice and Grace as Presented in Bergengruen's Fiction'. GR, vol. 31, 1956, pp. 97–103.

Kirchberger, Lida, 'Bergengruen's Novel of the Berlin Panic'. *Monatshefte*, vol. 46, 1954, pp. 199–206.

Peters, Eric, 'Werner Bergengruen. Realist and Mystic'. GLL, vol. 2, 1948–9, pp. 179–87.

BOBROWSKI, JOHANNES:

Bobrowski, Johannes, *Selbstzeugnisse und Beiträge über sein Werk*. Berlin, 1967.

Bridgwater, Patrick, 'The Poetry of Johannes Bobrowski'. FMLS, vol. 2, 1966, pp. 320–34.

Haufe, Eberhard, 'Bobrowskis Weg zum Roman. Zur Vor- und Entstehungsgeschichte von *Levins Mühle*'. *Weimarer Beiträge*, vol. 16, 1970, pp. 163–77.

Keith-Smith, Brian, *Johannes Bobrowski*, 1970.

Waidson, H. M., 'Bobrowski's *Levins Mühle*'. In: *Essays in German Language, Culture and Society*, ed. Siegbert S. Prawer, R. Hinton Thomas, Leonard Forster, 1969, pp. 149–59.

BÖLL, HEINRICH:

Bronsen, David, 'Böll's Women: Patterns in Male-Female Relationships'. *Monatshefte*, vol. 57, 1965, pp. 291–300.

Coupe, W. A., 'Heinrich Böll's *Und sagte kein einziges Wort*—An Analysis'. GLL, vol. 17, 1963–4, pp. 238–49.

Hanson, W. P., 'Heinrich Böll: *Das Brot der frühen Jahre*'. ML, vol. 48, 1967, pp. 148–51.

Klieneberger, H. R., 'Heinrich Böll in *Ansichten eines Clowns*'. GLL, vol. 19, 1965–6, pp. 34–9.

Lengning, Werner (ed.), *Der Schriftsteller Heinrich Böll. Ein biographisch-bibliographischer Abriß*. New edition, Munich, 1968 (first published Cologne and Berlin, 1959).

Paslick, Robert H., 'A Defense of Existence: Böll's *Ansichten eines Clowns*'. GQ, vol. 41, 1968, pp. 698–710.

Plant, Richard, 'The World of Heinrich Böll'. GQ, vol. 33, 1960, pp. 125–31.

Plard, Henri, 'Böll le constructeur: remarques sur *Billard um halbzehn*'. EG, vol. 15, 1960, pp. 120–43.

—— 'Heinrich Böll: The Author and his Works'. *Universitas (Quarterly English Language Edition)*, vol. 8, 1965, pp. 45–54.

Reid, James H., 'The Problem of Tradition in the Works of Heinrich Böll'. Dissertation Glasgow, 1966.

—— 'Time in the Works of Heinrich Böll'. MLR, vol. 62, 1967, pp. 476–85.

Sokel, Walter Herbert, 'Perspective and Dualism in the Novels of Böll'. In: Heitner, Robert R. (ed.), *The Contemporary Novel in German*, pp. 9–35.

Waidson, H. M., 'The Novels and Stories of Heinrich Böll'. GLL, vol. 12, 1958–9, pp. 264–72.

—— Introduction to edition (with Seidmann, Gertrud) of '*Doktor Murkes gesammeltes Schweigen*' *and Other Stories*, 1963.

Yuill, W. E., 'Heinrich Böll'. In: *Essays on Contemporary German Literature*, ed. Brian Keith-Smith, 1966, pp. 141–58.

Ziolkowski, Theodore, 'Albert Camus and Heinrich Böll'. MLN, vol. 77, 1962, pp. 282–91.

—— 'Heinrich Böll: Conscience and Craft.' BA, vol. 34, 1960, pp. 213–22.

BORCHERT, WOLFGANG:

Fickert, Kurt J., 'Some Biblical Prototypes in Wolfgang Borchert's Stories'. GQ, vol. 38, 1965, pp. 172–8.

Klarmann, Adolf D., 'Wolfgang Borchert: The Lost Voice of a New Germany'. GR, vol. 27, 1952, pp. 108–23.

Mileck, Joseph, 'Wolfgang Borchert: Bibliography'. GQ, vol. 33, 1960, pp. 233–9.

Popper, Hans, 'Wolfgang Borchert'. In: *German Men of Letters*, vol. 3, ed. Alex Natan, 1964, pp. 269–303.

Salmon, P. B., Introduction to edition of Borchert, *Draußen vor der Tür*, 1963.

Spaethling, Robert H., 'Wolfgang Borchert's Quest for Human Freedom'. GLL, vol. 14, 1961, pp. 188–93.

BRECHT, BERTOLT:

Esslin, Martin, *Brecht. A Choice of Evils*. 1959.

Gray, Ronald, *Brecht*. 1961.

Willett, John, *The Theatre of Bertolt Brecht*. 1959.

BREDEL, WILLI:

Andrews, R. C., 'The Novel as a Political Vade-Mecum: Willi Bredel's *Verwandte und Bekannte*'. GLL, vol. 10, 1956–7, pp. 131–8.

BROCH, HERMANN:

Cohn, Dorrit, 'Laughter at the Nadir: On a Theme in Hermann Broch's Novels'. *Monatshefte*, vol. 61, 1969, pp. 113–21.

Durzak, Manfred, *Hermann Broch*. Stuttgart, 1967.

—— 'Hermann Broch und James Joyce. Zur Ästhetik des modernen Romans'. DVjs, vol. 40, 1966, pp. 391–433.

Hardin, James N., '*Der Versucher* and Hermann Broch's Attitude towards Positivism'. GQ, vol. 39, 1966, pp. 29–41.

Herd, E. W., 'Hermann Broch and the Legitimacy of the Novel'. GLL, vol. 13, 1959–60, pp. 262–77.

—— 'The Guilt of the Hero in the Novels of Hermann Broch'. GLL, vol. 18, 1964–5, pp. 30–9.

Weigand, Hermann, 'Hermann Broch's *Die Schuldlosen*. An Approach'. PMLA, vol. 68, 1953, pp. 323–34.

—— 'Broch's *Death of Virgil*: Program Notes'. PMLA, vol. 62, 1947, pp. 525–54.

White, John J., 'Broch, Virgil, and the Cycle of History'. GR, vol. 41, 1966, pp. 103–10.

Ziolkowski, Theodore, *Hermann Broch*. New York and London, 1964.

CAROSSA, HANS:

Baier, C., Introduction to edition of *Selections from Hans Carossa*, 1960.

Bithell, Jethro, Introduction to edition of *Eine Kindheit*, Oxford, 1942.

—— 'Hans Carossa'. GLL, vol. 2, 1948–9, pp. 30–41.

Herd, E. W., 'The dream-motif in the work of Hans Carossa'. GLL, vol. 4, 1951, pp. 171–5.

Hofacker, Erich, 'Recollection and Reality in Carossa's Autobiography'. *Monatshefte*, vol. 42, 1950, pp. 89–95.

Subiotto, A. V., 'Hans Carossa'. GLL, vol. 11, 1957–8, pp. 34–40.

DÖBLIN, ALFRED:

Casey, Timothy Joseph, 'Alfred Döblin'. In: *Expressionismus als Literatur*, ed. Wolfgang Rothe, Berne and Munich, 1969, pp. 637–55.

Reid, James H., 'Berlin Alexanderplatz—A Political Novel'. GLL, vol. 21, 1967–8, pp. 214–23.

Strelka, Joseph, 'Der Erzähler Alfred Döblin'. GQ, vol. 33, 1960, pp. 197–210.

DODERER, HEIMITO VON:

Hayward-Jones, Sylvia, 'Fate, Guilt and Freedom in Heimito von Doderer's *Ein Mord, den jeder begeht* and *Ein Umweg*'. GLL, vol. 14, 1960–1, pp. 160–4.

Ivask, Ivar (ed.), 'An International Symposium in Memory of Heimito von Doderer (1896–1966)'. BA, vol. 42, 1968, pp. 343–84.

Mitchell, M. R., 'Heimito von Doderer as a Social Novelist'. Dissertation Oxford, 1970.

Politzer, Heinz, 'Heimito von Doderer's *Demons* and the Modern Kakanian Novel'. In: Heitner, Robert R. (ed.), *The Contemporary Novel in German*, pp. 37–62.

Seidmann, Gertrud, 'Heimito von Doderer'. ML, vol. 40, 1959, pp. 53–6.

Swales, M. W., 'The Narrator in the Novels of Heimito von Doderer'. MLR, vol. 61, 1966, pp. 85–95.

—— 'Ordnung und Verworrenheit. Zum Werk Heimito von Doderers'. WW, vol. 18, 1968, pp. 96–130.

Waidson, H. M., 'Heimito von Doderer's Demons'. GLL, vol. 11, 1957–8, pp. 214–24.

Weber, Dietrich, *Heimito von Doderer*. Munich, 1963.

DÜRRENMATT, FRIEDRICH:

Alexander, F. J., Introduction to edition of *Die Panne* and *Der Tunnel*, Oxford, 1967.

Brock-Sulzer, Elisabeth, *Dürrenmatt. Stationen seines Werkes*. Zürich, 1960.

Diller, Edward, 'Friedrich Dürrenmatt's Theological Concept of History'. GQ, vol. 40, 1967, pp. 363–71.

Forster, Leonard, Introductions to editions of *Der Richter und sein Henker*, 1962, *Der Verdacht*, 1965, *Das Versprechen*, 1967.

Gillis, William, 'Dürrenmatt and the Detectives'. GQ, vol. 35, 1962, pp. 71–4.

Gontrum, Peter B., '*Ritter, Tod und Teufel*: Protagonists and Antagonists in the Prose Works of Friedrich Dürrenmatt'. *Seminar*, vol. 1, 1965, pp. 88–98.

Hansel, Johannes, *Friedrich-Dürrenmatt-Bibliographie*. Bad Homburg, Berlin and Zürich, 1968.

Johnson, Peter, 'Grotesqueness and Injustice in Dürrenmatt'. GLL, vol. 15, 1961–2, pp. 264–73.

Leah, Gordon N., 'Dürrenmatt's Detective Stories'. ML, vol. 48, 1967, pp. 65–9.

Waidson, H. M., 'Friedrich Dürrenmatt'. In: *Swiss Men of Letters*, ed. Alex Natan, 1970, pp. 261–86.

EDSCHMID, KASIMIR:

Brammer, Ursula G., 'Kasimir Edschmid. Eine Bibliographie'. MLN, vol. 84, 1969, pp. 415–40.

Weltmann, Lutz, 'Kasimir Edschmid'. GLL, vol. 1, 1947–8, pp. 312–19.

FRISCH, MAX:

Barlow, D., '"Ordnung" and "Das Wirkliche Leben" in the Work of Max Frisch'. GLL, vol. 19, 1965–6, pp. 52–60.

Bradley, Brigitte L., 'Max Frisch's *Homo Faber*: Theme and Structural Devices'. GR, vol. 41, 1966, pp. 279–90.

Cock, Mary E., '"Countries of the Mind": Max Frisch's Narrative Technique'. MLR, vol. 65, 1970, pp. 820–8.

Cunliffe, W. G., 'Existentialist Elements in Frisch's Works'. *Monatshefte*, vol. 62, 1970, pp. 113–22.

Esslin, Martin, 'Max Frisch'. In: *Swiss Men of Letters*, ed. Alex Natan, 1970, pp. 241–58.

Hoffmann, Charles W., 'The Search for Self, Inner Freedom, and

Relatedness in the Novels of Max Frisch'. In: Heitner, Robert R. (ed.), *The Contemporary Novel in German*, pp. 91–113.

Manger, Philip, 'Kierkegaard in Max Frisch's Novel *Stiller*'. GLL, vol. 20, 1966–7, pp. 119–31.

Marchand, Wolf R., 'Max Frisch, *Mein Name sei Gantenbein*'. ZDP, vol. 87, 1968, pp. 510–35.

White, Andrew, 'Labyrinths of Modern Fiction. Max Frisch's *Stiller* as a Novel of Alienation, and the "Nouveau roman"'. *Arcadia*, vol. 2, 1967, pp. 288–304.

GAISER, GERD:

Bronsen, David, 'Unterdrückung und Pathos in Gerd Gaisers *Die sterbende Jagd*'. GQ, vol. 38, 1965, pp. 310–17.

Bullivant, K., Introduction to edition of Gaiser, *Am Paß Nascondo und andere Erzählungen*, 1968.

Hilton, Ian, 'Gerd Gaiser'. In: *Essays on Contemporary German Literature*, ed. Brian Keith-Smith, 1966, pp. 111–38.

Hohoff, Curt, *Gerd Gaiser, Werk und Gestalt*. Munich, 1962.

Stutz, Elfriede, 'Über die Sprache Gerd Gaisers'. DU, vol. 15, no. 3, 1963, pp. 70–82.

GOES, ALBRECHT:

Fitzell, John, 'Albrecht Goes: The Poet as Spiritual Guest'. *Monatshefte*, vol. 50, 1958, pp. 348–58.

Robinson, Alan R., Introduction to edition of *Das Brandopfer*, 1958.

Trainer, J., 'Two Prose Works of Albrecht Goes'. ML, vol. 42, 1961, pp. 137–9.

GRAF, OSKAR MARIA:

Pfanner, Helmut F., 'Oskar Maria Graf: Ein Überblick über sein literarisches Werk'. *Seminar*, vol. 6, 1970, pp. 195–206.

GRASS, GÜNTER:

Abbé, Derek Van, 'Metamorphoses of "Unbewältigte Vergangenheit" in *Die Blechtrommel*'. GLL, vol. 23, 1970, pp. 152–60.

Andrews, R. C., 'The Tin Drum'. ML, vol. 45, 1964, pp. 28–31.

Bance, A. F., 'The enigma of Oskar in Grass's *Blechtrommel*'. *Seminar*, vol. 3, 1967, pp. 147–56.

Behrendt, Johanna E., 'Die Ausweglosigkeit der menschlichen Natur. Eine Interpretation von Günter Grass' *Katz und Maus*'. ZDP, vol. 87, 1968, pp. 546–62.

Boa, Elizabeth, 'Günter Grass and the German Gremlin'. GLL, vol. 23, 1970, pp. 144–51.

Bruce, James C., 'The Equivocating Narrator in Günter Grass's *Katz und Maus*'. *Monatshefte*, vol. 58, 1966, pp. 139–49.

Friedrichsmeyer, Erhard M., 'Aspects of Myth, Parody, and Obscenity in Grass's *Die Blechtrommel* and *Katz und Maus*'. GR, vol. 40, 1965, pp. 240–50.

Gelley, Alexander, 'Art and Reality in *Die Blechtrommel*'. FMLS, vol. 3, 1967, pp. 115–25.

Hatfield, Henry, 'Günter Grass: The Artist as Satirist'. In: Heitner, Robert R., (ed.), *The Contemporary Novel in German*, pp. 115–34.

Parry, Idris, 'Aspects of Günter Grass's Narrative Technique'. FMLS, vol. 3, 1967, pp. 99–114.

Spaethling, Robert H., 'Günter Grass: *Cat and Mouse*'. *Monatshefte*, vol. 62, 1970, pp. 141–53.

Subiotto, Arrigo, 'Günter Grass'. In: *Essays on Contemporary German Literature*, ed. Brian Keith-Smith, 1966, pp. 215–58.

Tank, Kurt Lothar, *Günter Grass*. Berlin, 1965.

Willson, A. Leslie, 'The Grotesque Everyman in Günter Grass's *Die Blechtrommel*'. *Monatshefte*, vol. 58, 1966, pp. 131–8.

GÜTERSLOH, ALBERT PARIS:
Doderer, Heimito von, and others, *Albert Paris Gütersloh. Autor und Werk*. Munich, 1962.

HEISELER, BERNDT VON:
Closs, A., 'Berndt von Heiseler's *Versöhnung*'. GLL, vol. 7, 1953–4, pp. 293–5.

HILDESHEIMER, WOLFGANG:
Kähler, Hermann, 'Hildesheimers Flucht nach Tynset'. *Sinn und Form*, vol. 17, 1965, pp. 792–7.

INGLIN, MEINRAD:
Wilhelm, Egon, *Meinrad Inglin*. Zürich and Freiburg i.B., 1957.

JAHNN, HANS HENNY:
Marr, Weaver M., 'Compassion and the Outsider: Hans Henny Jahnn's *Die Nacht aus Blei*'. GR, vol. 39, 1964, pp. 201–10.

Meyer, Jochen, *Verzeichnis der Schriften von und über Hans Henny Jahnn*. Neuwied and Berlin, 1967.

JENS, WALTER:
Just, Gottfried, and others, *Walter Jens. Eine Einführung*. Munich, 1965.

JOHNSON, UWE:

Detweiler, Robert, '*Speculations about Jacob*: The Truth of Ambiguity'. *Monatshefte*, vol. 58, 1966, pp. 24–32.

Friedrichsmeyer, Erhard, 'Quest by Supposition: Johnson's *Mutmaßungen über Jakob*'. GR, vol. 42, 1967, pp. 215–26.

Migner, Karl, 'Uwe Johnson: *Das dritte Buch über Achim*'. DU, vol. 16, no. 2, 1964, pp. 17–25.

JÜNGER, ERNST:

Friedrich, Gerhard, 'Ernst Jünger: *Auf den Marmorklippen*'. DU, vol. 16, no. 2, 1964, pp. 41–52.

Hafkesbrink, Hanna, 'Ernst Jünger's Quest for a New Faith'. GR, vol. 26, 1951, pp. 289–300.

Peppard, Murray B., 'Ernst Jünger: Norse Myths and Nihilism'. *Monatshefte*, vol. 46, pp. 1–10.

Rey, W. H., 'Ernst Jünger and the Crisis of Civilization'. GLL, vol. 5, 1951–2, pp. 249–54.

Stern, J. P., *Ernst Jünger, A Writer of Our Time*. Cambridge, 1953.

KASACK, HERMANN:

Anderle, Martin, 'Mensch und Architektur im Werk Hermann Kasacks'. GQ, vol. 38, 1965, pp. 20–9.

Kasack, Wolfgang (ed.), *Leben und Werk von Hermann Kasack. Ein Brevier*. Frankfurt am Main, 1966.

Mainland, W. F., 'Hermann Kasack'. In: *Essays on Contemporary German Literature*, ed. Brian Keith-Smith. 1966, pp. 39–59.

KOEPPEN, WOLFGANG (and ANDERSCH, ALFRED):

Bance, A. F., '*Der Tod in Rom* and *Die Rote*: Two Italian Episodes'. FMLS, vol. 3, 1967, pp. 126–34.

Bungter, Georg, 'Über Wolfgang Koeppens *Tauben im Gras*'. ZDP, vol. 87, 1968, pp. 535–45.

KREUDER, ERNST:

Girault, Claude, 'Ernst Kreuder ou l'écrivain et la réalité'. EG, vol. 12, 1957, pp. 209–39.

LAMPE, FRIEDO:

Thomas, Lionel, 'Friedo Lampe and his Work—An Introduction'. GLL, vol. 14, 1960–1, pp. 194–203.

LANGGÄSSER, ELISABETH:

Hautumm, Hans-Ludwig, 'Das Selbstverständnis der Dichtung bei Elisabeth Langgässer'. DU, vol. 16, no. 5, 1964, pp. 34–49.

Neuschaffer, W., 'Elisabeth Langgässer'. ML, vol. 36, 1954–5, pp. 18–21.

Politzer, Heinz, 'The Indelible Seal of Elisabeth Langgässer'. GR, vol. 27, 1952, pp. 200–9.

Riley, Anthony W., 'Die Literatur über Elisabeth Langgässer: Eine Bibliographie'. *Literaturwissenschaftliches Jahrbuch im Auftrage der Görres-Gesellschaft*, New Series, vol. 8, 1967, pp. 265–87.

—— (in collaboration with Grüttner-Hoffmann, Barbara), 'Das Werk Elisabeth Langgässers: Eine Bibliographie'. *Literaturwissenschaftliches Jahrbuch im Auftrage der Görres-Gesellschaft*, New Series, vol. 9, 1968, pp. 333–62.

Theunissen, Gert H., 'The Way Out of the Wilderness'. GLL, vol. 2, 1948–9, pp. 194–200.

LE FORT, GERTRUD VON:

Foster, J. R., Introduction to edition of Le Fort, *Am Tor des Himmels*, 1966.

Hilton, Ian, 'Gertrud von le Fort—a Christian Writer'. GLL, vol. 15, 1961–2, pp. 300–8.

—— 'Gertrud von le Fort'. In: *German Men of Letters*, vol. 2, ed. Alex Natan. 1963, pp. 277–98.

Neuschaffer, W., 'The World of Gertrud von le Fort'. GLL, vol. 8, 1954–5, pp. 30–6.

O'Boyle, Ita, *Gertrud von le Fort. An Introduction to the Prose Work*. Fordham, 1964.

Wunderlich, Eva C., 'Gertrud von le Fort's Fight for the Living Spirit'. GR, vol. 27, 1952, pp. 298–313.

LENZ, SIEGFRIED:

Just, Klaus Günther, 'Siegfried Lenz als Erzähler'. WW, vol. 16, 1966, pp. 112–24.

Prager, P., Introduction to edition of Lenz, *Zeit der Schuldlosen*, 1966.

Russ, C. A. H., 'The Short Stories of Siegfried Lenz'. GLL, vol. 19, 1965–6, pp. 241–51.

LERNET-HOLENIA, ALEXANDER:

Bednall, J. B., 'Alexander Lernet-Holenia'. ML, vol. 43, 1962, pp. 28–31.

MANN, HEINRICH:

Weisstein, Ulrich, 'Heinrich Mann in America: A Critical Survey'. BA, vol. 33, 1959, pp. 281–4.

Yuill, W. E., 'Heinrich Mann'. In: *German Men of Letters*, vol. 2, ed. Alex Natan, 1963, pp. 199–224.

MANN, THOMAS:

Brandt, Thomas O., 'Narcissism in Thomas Mann's *Der Erwählte*'. GLL, vol. 7, 1953–4, pp. 233–41.

Eichner, Hans, 'The Place of *Doktor Faustus* in the Work of Thomas Mann'. GLL, vol. 1, 1947–8, pp. 289–302.

Fürstenheim, E. G., 'The Place of *Der Erwählte* in the Work of Thomas Mann'. MLR, vol. 51, 1956, pp. 55–70.

Gray, R. D., 'Alleluia on a Toy Trumpet'. GLL, vol. 5, 1951–2, pp. 57–61.

Gronicka, André von, 'Thomas Mann's *Doktor Faustus*', GR, vol. 23, 1948, pp. 206–18.

Heller, Erich, *The Ironic German: A Study of Thomas Mann*. 1958.

Jonas, Klaus W., *Fifty Years of Thomas Mann Studies*. Minneapolis, 1956.

Jonas, Klaus W. and Jonas, Ilsedore B., *Thomas Mann Studies*, Volume II, *A Bibliography of Criticism*. Philadelphia, 1967.

Maier, Hans Albert, 'Die Stellung des *Doktor Faustus* im Gesamtwerke Thomas Manns'. MLQ, vol. 9, 1948, pp. 343–53.

McClain, William H., 'Irony and Belief in Thomas Mann's *Der Erwählte*'. *Monatshefte*, vol. 43, 1951, pp. 319–23.

Parry, Idris, 'Thomas Mann's Latest Phase'. GLL, vol. 8, 1954–5, pp. 241–51.

Schoolfield, George C., 'Thomas Mann's *Die Betrogene*'. GR, vol. 38, 1963, pp. 91–120.

Stein, Jack M., 'Adrian Leverkühn as a Composer'. GR, vol. 25, 1950, pp. 257–74.

Thomas, R. Hinton, *Thomas Mann. The Mediation of Art*. Oxford, 1956.

Tuska, Jon, 'The Vision of Doktor Faustus'. GR, vol. 40, 1965, pp. 277–309.

Weigand, Hermann J., 'Thomas Mann's Gregorius'. GR, vol. 37, 1952, pp. 10–30, 83–95.

White, Andrew, *Thomas Mann*. Edinburgh and London, 1965.

Williams, W. D., 'Thomas Mann's *Dr. Faustus*'. GLL, vol. 12, 1958–9, pp. 273–81.

NOLL, DIETER:

Geerdts, Hans Jürgen, 'Die Schicksalsfrage Büchners neu gestellt. Bemerkungen zu Nolls Roman *Die Abenteuer des Werner Holt*'. *Weimarer Beiträge*, vol. 11, 1965, pp. 147–58.

NOSSACK, HANS ERICH:

Biser, Eugen, 'Der Wegbereiter. Zur Gestalt des Engels im Werk Hans Erich Nossacks'. DU, vol. 16, no. 5, 1964, pp. 22–33.

Friedrich, Gerhard, 'Mensch und Wirklichkeit im Werk Hans Erich Nossacks'. DU, vol. 15, no. 3, 1963, pp. 48–58.

Goerke, Hans, 'Hans Erich Nossack: *Der Untergang*'. DU, vol. 15, no. 3, 1963, pp. 59–69.

Hubsch, Peter, 'Hans Erich Nossack'. *Germania*, vol. 5, 1969, pp. 12–15.

—— 'The Theme of Identity in the Works of Hans Erich Nossack'. Dissertation Swansea, 1968.

Keith-Smith, Brian, 'Hans Erich Nossack'. In: *Essays on Contemporary German Literature*, ed. Brian Keith-Smith, 1966, pp. 63–85.

Plard, Henri, 'La jeune fille et la mort: *Das kennt man*, de Hans Erich Nossack'. EG, vol. 23, 1968, pp. 12–36.

Prochnik, Peter, 'Controlling Thoughts in the Work of Hans Erich Nossack'. GLL, vol. 19, 1965–6, pp. 68–74.

Puppe, Heinz W., 'Hans Erich Nossack und der Nihilismus'. GQ, vol. 37, 1964, pp. 1–16.

RINSER, LUISE:

Scholz, Albert, *Luise Rinsers Leben und Werk. Eine Einführung*. Syracuse, N.Y., 1968.

RISSE, HEINZ:

Heinz Risse 70 Jahre. Krefeld, 1968.

Hubbs, Valentine C., 'The Worlds of Heinz Risse'. BA, vol. 37, 1963, pp. 138–43.

SCHAPER, EDZARD:

Besch, Lutz, *Gespräche mit Edzard Schaper*. Zürich, 1968.

Guder, G., 'Edzard Schaper'. ML, vol. 38, 1957, pp. 61–5.

Jepson, J. E., 'Edzard Schaper's Image of Man and Society in the *Gesammelte Erzählungen*'. GLL, vol. 23, 1970, pp. 323–31.

SCHMIDT, ARNO:

Schmidt-Henkel, Gerhard, 'Arno Schmidt und seine *Gelehrtenrepublik*.' ZDP, vol. 87, 1968, pp. 563–91.

SEGHERS, ANNA:

Andrews, R. C., 'An East German Novelist: Anna Seghers'. GLL, vol. 8, 1954–5, pp. 121–9.

—— 'Anna Seghers's *Die Entscheidung*'. GLL, vol. 15, 1961–2, pp. 259–63.

Haas, Gerhard, 'Veränderung und Dauer. Anna Seghers: *Das siebte Kreuz*'. DU, vol. 20, no. 1, 1968, pp. 43–56.

Neugebauer, Heinz, *Anna Seghers*, Berlin, 1962.

SEIDEL, INA:

Foulger, L. E., 'The Prose Works of Ina Seidel' Dissertation Leeds, 1970.

Horst, Karl August, *Ina Seidel. Wesen und Werk*. Stuttgart, 1956.

STRITTMATTER, ERWIN:

Thalheim, Hans-Günther, 'Zur Entwicklung des epischen Helden und zum Problem des Menschenbildes in Erwin Strittmatters *Ole Bienkopp*'. *Weimarer Beiträge*, vol. 10, 1964, pp. 228–34 and 501–24.

WALSER, MARTIN:

Andrews, R. C., 'Comedy and Satire in Martin Walser's *Halbzeit*'. ML, vol. 50, 1969, pp. 6–10.

Beckermann, Thomas (ed.), *Über Martin Walser*. Frankfurt, 1970.

Nelson, Donald F., 'The Depersonalized World of Martin Walser'. GQ, vol. 42, 1969, pp. 204–16.

Stubbs, A. E., 'Martin Walser's Fiction, 1955–1966'. Dissertation Southampton, 1970.

WEISS, PETER:

Hilton, Ian, *Peter Weiss. A Search for Affinities*, 1970.

Milfull, John, 'From Kafka to Brecht: Peter Weiss's Development towards Marxism'. GLL, vol. 20, 1966–7, pp. 61–71.

Zeller, Rose, 'Peter Weiss *Der Schatten des Körpers des Kutschers*. Erzähler und Autor'. ZDP, vol. 87, 1968, pp. 643–60.

WERFEL, FRANZ:

Fox, W. H., 'Franz Werfel'. In: *German Men of Letters*, vol. 3, ed. Alex Natan, 1964, pp. 107–25.

Klarmann, Adolf D., 'Franz Werfel's Eschatology and Cosmogony'. MLQ, vol. 7, 1946, pp. 385–410.

Puttkamer, Annemarie von, *Franz Werfel. Wort und Antwort*. Würzburg, 1952.

WIECHERT, ERNST:

Berger, Walter, 'Ernst Wiechert'. GLL, vol. 4, 1950–1, pp. 11–20.

Chick, Edson M., 'Ernst Wiechert and the Problem of Evil'. *Monatshefte*, vol. 46, 1954, pp. 181–91.

Frey, John R., 'The "Grim Reaper" in the Works of Ernst Wiechert'. *Monatshefte*, vol. 42, 1950, pp. 201–13.

Herd, E. W., 'The "Unpolitical" Outlook of Ernst Wiechert'. GLL, vol. 7, 1953–4, pp. 266–71.

Hollmann, Werner, 'Ethical Responsibility and Personal Freedom in the Works of Ernst Wiechert'. GR, vol. 25, 1950, pp. 37–49.

Puknat, Siegfried B., 'God, Man and Society in the Recent Fiction of Ernst Wiechert'. GLL, vol. 3, 1949–50, pp. 221–30.

—— 'Wiechert Bibliography'. *Monatshefte*, vol. 43, 1951, pp. 409–13.

WOLF, CHRISTA:

Kloehn, Ekkehard, 'Christa Wolf: *Der geteilte Himmel*'. DU, vol. 20, no. 1, 1968, pp. 43–56.

Schlenstedt, Dieter, 'Motive und Symbole in Christa Wolfs Erzählung *Der geteilte Himmel*'. *Weimarer Beiträge*, vol. 10, 1964, pp. 77–104.

ZUCKMAYER, CARL:

Barlow, D., Introduction to edition of Zuckmayer, *Three Stories*. Oxford, 1963.

Robinson, Alan R., Introduction to edition of Zuckmayer, *Der Seelenbräu*, 1960.

Rooke, Sheila, 'Carl Zuckmayer'. In: *German Men of Letters*, vol. 3, ed. Alex Natan, 1964, pp. 209–33.

ZWEIG, ARNOLD:

Hilscher, Eberhard, *Arnold Zweig, Leben und Werk*. Berlin, 1968.

LIST OF TRANSLATIONS

This check-list is in general restricted to English translations of prose narrative works mentioned in the preceding pages which were first published in German between 1945 and 1965. The name of the translator is given after the title. For further information reference may be made to such works as the *British National Bibliography* or *Translations from the German: English 1948–1964* (ed. Richard Mönnig).

Aichinger, Ilse, *The Bound Man and Other Stories*, Eric Mosbacher, 1955.
Andersch, Alfred, *Flight to Afar*, Michael Bullock, 1958.
—— *The Night of the Giraffe and Other Stories*, Christa Armstrong, 1964.
—— *The Redhead*, Michael Bullock, 1961.
Andres, Stefan, *We Are Utopia*, Cyrus Brooks, 1954.
Apitz, Bruno, *Naked among Wolves*, Edith Anderson, 1960.
Benn, Gottfried, *Primal Vision. Selected Writings*, E. B. Ashton and others, 1960.
Bergengruen, Werner, *The Last Captain of Horse. A Portrait of Chivalry*, Eric Peters, 1953.
Bobrowski, Johannes, *Levin's Mill*, Janet Cooper, 1970.
Böll, Heinrich, *Absent without Leave and Other Stories*, Leila Vennewitz, 1967.
—— *Acquainted with the Night*, Richard Graves, 1955.
—— *Adam, Where Art Thou?*, Mervyn Savill, 1955.
—— *Billiards at Half Past Nine*, Patrick Bowles, 1961.
—— *The Bread of Our Early Years*, Mervyn Savill, 1957.
—— *The Clown*, Leila Vennewitz, 1965.
—— *The End of a Mission*, Leila Vennewitz, 1968.
—— *The Train Was on Time*, Richard Graves, 1956.
—— *Traveller, if You Come to Spa—*, Mervyn Savill, 1950.
—— *The Unguarded House*, Mervyn Savill, 1957.
Borchert, Wolfgang, *The Man Outside. The Prose Works of Wolfgang Borchert*, David Porter, 1952.
Brecht, Bertolt, *Tales from the Calendar*, Yvonne Kapp and Michael Hamburger, 1961.

Broch, Hermann, *The Death of Virgil*, Jean Starr Untermeyer, 1945.

Doderer, Heimito von, *The Demons*, Richard and Clara Winston, 1961.

Dürrenmatt, Friedrich, *A Dangerous Game*, Richard and Clara Winston, 1960.

—— *The Judge and his Hangman*, Cyrus Brooks, 1954.

—— *Once a Greek . . .*, Richard and Clara Winston, 1965.

—— *The Pledge*, Richard and Clara Winston, 1959.

—— *The Quarry*, Eva H. Morreale, 1962.

Frisch, Max, *Homo Faber, A Report*, Michael Bullock, 1959.

—— *I'm not Stiller*, Michael Bullock, 1958.

—— *A Wilderness of Mirrors*, Michael Bullock, 1965.

Gaiser, Gerd, *The Falling Leaf*, Paul Lindlay, 1956; also as *The Last Squadron*, 1960.

—— *The Last Dance of the Season*, Marguerite Waldman, 1960; also as *The Final Ball*, 1960.

Goes, Albrecht, *Arrow to the Heart*, Constantine Fitzgibbon, 1951, also as *Unquiet Night*, 1951.

—— *The Burnt Offering*, Michael Hamburger, 1956.

Grass, Günter, *Cat and Mouse*, Ralph Manheim, 1963.

—— *Dog Years*, Ralph Manheim, 1965.

—— *The Tin Drum*, Ralph Manheim, 1962.

Heinrich, Willi, *The Willing Flesh*, Richard and Clara Winston, 1956.

Jahnn, Hans Henny, *The Ship*, Catherine Hutter, 1961.

Jens, Walter, *The Blind Man*, Michael Bullock, 1954.

Johnson, Uwe, *Speculations about Jakob*, Ursule Molinaro, 1963.

—— *The Third Book about Achim*, Ursule Molinaro, 1964.

—— *Two Views*, Richard and Clara Winston, 1966.

Jünger, Ernst, *The Glass Bees*, Louise Bogan and Elizabeth Mayer, 1960.

Kasack, Hermann, *The City Beyond the River*, Peter de Mendelssohn, 1953.

Kirst, Hans Hellmut, *Zero Eight Fifteen. The Strange Mutiny of Gunner Asch*, Robert Kee, 1955.

—— *Zero Eight Fifteen, 2. Gunner Asch Goes to War*, Robert Kee, 1956.

—— *Zero Eight Fifteen, 3. The Return of Gunner Asch*, Robert Kee, 1957.

Koeppen, Wolfgang, *Death in Rome*, Mervyn Savill, 1956.

Kreuder, Ernst, *The Attic Pretenders*, Robert Kee, 1948.

Langgässer, Elisabeth, *The Quest*, J. B. Greene, 1953.

Ledig, Gert, *The Naked Hill*, Mervyn Savill, 1956.

Le Fort, Gertrud von, *The Wife of Pilate*, Marie C. Buehrle, 1957.

Lernet-Holenia, Alexander, *Count Luna*, Jane B. Greene; and *Baron Bagge*, Richard and Clara Winston, 1956.

Mann, Thomas, *The Black Swan*, Willard R. Trask, 1954.

—— *Confessions of Felix Krull, Confidence Man*, Denver Lindley, 1955.

—— *Doctor Faustus. The Life of the German Composer as Told by a Friend*, H. T. Lowe-Porter, 1948.

—— *The Holy Sinner*, H. T. Lowe-Porter, 1951.

Meichsner, Dieter, *Vain Glory*, Charlotte and A. L. Lloyd, 1953; also as *Answer in the Sky*.

Nossack, Hans Erich, *The Impossible Proof*, Michael Lebeck, 1968 (originally published as 'Unmögliche Beweisaufnahme' in *Spirale*, 1956).

Plievier, Theodor, *Berlin*, Louis Hagen and Vivian Milroy, 1956.

—— *Moscow*, Stuart Hood, 1953.

—— *Stalingrad, The Death of an Army*, H. Langmead Robinson, 1948.

Remarque, Erich Maria, *Arch of Triumph*, Walter Sorell and Denver Lindley, 1946.

—— *Heaven Has No Favourites*, Richard and Clara Winston, 1961.

—— *The Night in Lisbon*, Ralph Manheim, 1964.

Richter, Hans Werner, *The Odds against Us*, Robert Kee, 1950; also as *Beyond Defeat*, 1960.

—— *They Fell from God's Hand*, Geoffrey Sainsbury, 1956.

Rinser, Luise, *Nina*, Richard and Clara Winston, 1956.

Risse, Heinz, *The Earthquake*, Rita Eldon, 1953.

Seghers, Anna, *The Dead Stay Young*, 1950.

Walser, Martin, *The Gadarene Club*, Eva Figes, 1960; also as *Marriage in Philippsburg*.

Weiss, Peter, *Leavetaking* and *Vanishing Point*, Christopher Levenson, 1966.

Wiechert, Ernst, *The Earth Is our Heritage*, Robert Maxwell, 1951.

—— *Missa sine Nomine*, Marie Heynemann and Margery B. Ledward, 1950; also as *Tidings*, 1959.

Zuckmayer, Carl, *Carnival Confession*, John and Necke Mander, 1961.

Zweig, Arnold, *The Axe of Wandsbek*, Eric Sutton, 1948.

—— *The Time Is Ripe*, Kenneth Bannerji and Michael Wharton, 1962.

INDEX

Aichinger, Ilse, 107
Andersch, Alfred, 103, 107–9
Andres, Stefan, 49–51
Apitz, Bruno, 133–4
Auden, W. H., 59
Austen, Jane, 1

Becher, J. R., 129–30
Benn, Gottfried, 58–9, 75
Bergengruen, Werner, 38–41, 141, 142
Bernanos, Georges, 42, 46
Bobrowski, Johannes, 139–40
Boccaccio, Giovanni, 25
Böll, Heinrich, 104, 109–15, 143, 144
Borchert, Wolfgang, 82
Brecht, Bertolt, 44, 110, 135–6
Bredel, Willi, 130
Broch, Hermann, 9, 10, 12, 26–9, 35, 63, 76, 87, 128
Burckhardt, C. J., 97

Carossa, Hans, 53–4, 95
Chesterton, G. K., 50

Dickens, Charles, 1, 50, 110
Diderot, Denis, 110
Döblin, Alfred, 9–10, 12, 24–6, 57
Doderer, Heimito von, 12, 63–8
Dos Passos, John, 9, 25
Dostoievsky, Fyodor, 17
Dürrenmatt, Friedrich, 97–9

Edschmid, Kasimir (Schmid, Eduard), 57–8
Eliot, T. S., 59
Ernst, Fritz, 93

Faulkner, William, 46
Forster, E. M., 71
Freud, Sigmund, 2, 7, 8
Frisch, Max, 97, 99–102, 145

Gaiser, Gerd, 86–8, 145–6
Goes, Albrecht, 80

Goethe, J. W. von, 3, 12, 14, 18, 25, 26, 109, 121, 143
Gotthelf, Jeremias (Bitzius, Albert), 28, 56, 95, 97
Graf, O. M., 30–2, 136
Grass, Günter, 121–3, 144, 145
Greene, Graham, 46, 78, 100
Guggenheim, Kurt, 96–7
Gütersloh, Albert Paris (Kiehtreiber, Albert Conrad), 68–9

Hardy, Thomas, 56
Heinrich, Willi, 85
Heiseler, Bernt von, 56–7
Hemingway, Ernest, 83, 100, 104
Hesse, Hermann, 7–9, 29, 74, 93, 104, 106
Hesse, M. R., 59–60, 95
Heuschele, Otto, 56
Hildesheimer, Wolfgang, 116
Hoffmann, E. T. A., 39
Hofmannsthal, Hugo von, 5, 97, 109
Huch, Ricarda, 42
Huxley, Aldous, 29

Ihlenfeld, Kurt, 80–2
Inglin, Meinrad, 93–5

Jahnn, H. H., 34–7
James, Henry, 1, 4
Jens, Walter, 101, 105–6
Johnson, Uwe, 123–5, 138, 144
Joyce, James, 3, 4, 9, 26, 27, 46, 66, 78
Jung, C. G., 8
Jünger, Ernst, 61–3, 100, 141

Kafka, Franz, 3, 6–7, 73, 100, 104, 106, 142
Kasack, Hermann, 73–4, 106
Keller, Gottfried, 95, 96
Kesten, Hermann, 32–3, 104
Kirst, H. H., 85
Kleist, Heinrich von, 40, 80
Klepper, Jochen, 80
Koeppen, Wolfgang, 90–2, 144

Index

Krämer-Badoni, Rudolf, 84–5
Kreuder, Ernst, 77–80
Kübler, Alfred, 95–6

Lampe, Friedo, 77
Landgrebe, Erich, 85
Langgässer, Elisabeth, 45–7, 76
Lawrence, D. H., 83
Le Fort, Gertrud von, 41–5, 54, 141, 142
Lenz, Siegfried, 116–19, 145
Lernet-Holenia, Alexander, 60–1
Lettau, Reinhard, 103

Mann, Heinrich, 12, 15, 23–4, 134
Mann, Thomas, 2, 3, 4, 12, 14–23, 35, 91, 100, 104, 109, 134, 141
Meichsner, Dieter, 83
Meyer, C. F., 42
Mörike, Eduard, 80
Musil, Robert, 9, 10–11, 12, 63, 66, 128

Nietzsche, Friedrich, 14, 18, 19, 42, 43
Noll, Dieter, 137–8
Nossack, H. E., 70–3

Orwell, George (Blair, Eric), 106

Paul, Jean (Richter, J. P. F.), 78
Plievier, Theodor, 33–4, 85
Proust, Marcel, 3, 4, 66

Remarque, E. M., 33
Richter, H. W., 103, 104–5, 134, 143
Rilke, R. M., 5–6, 42, 143
Rinser, Luise, 83–4
Risse, Heinz, 74–6
Romains, Jules, 9, 25

Schaper, Edzard, 51–3, 144
Schmidt, Arno, 88–90, 144
Schnurre, Wolfdietrich, 115–16
Schröers, Rolf, 104
Seidel, Ina, 47–9
Seghers, Anna (Radvanyi, Netty), 131–3, 145
Shakespeare, William, 3
Shaw, G. B., 50
Stein, Gertrude, 90
Stephan, Hanna, 56
Stifter, Adalbert, 12
Strittmatter, Erwin, 136–7

Thackeray, W. M., 1
Thomas, Dylan, 108
Tolstoy, Leo, 14, 131

Uhse, Bodo, 130–1

Voltaire, F. M. A. de, 75

Wagner, Richard, 14, 19
Walser, Martin, 119–20, 144
Walser, Robert, 77, 93
Walter, Hans, 97
Warsinsky, Werner, 76–7
Weiss, Peter, 125–7
Werfel, Franz, 29–30, 106
Wiechert, Ernst, 55–6, 141
Wolf, Christa, 138–9
Woolf, Virginia, 3

Zuckmayer, Carl, 30
Zweig, Arnold, 128–9, 130, 145